'Desirability equals disposability: it is ........
diabolical logic that global digital cap............
lives to market in myriad ways that have ..... ..... been familiar
to the most marginalized among us. At the same time, the
deep technological interconnectedness of contemporary
human lives offers new possibilities for redistribution, com-
munisation and "unwork". How can today's Bartlebys, in
solidarity with each other's desires, rebuild the ability to say
"I would prefer not to" together on this terrain and, going
beyond that, determine what it is we want? Combining an
unprecedented overview of contemporary paradoxes in the
politics of anti-work with a fresh and sophisticated argument for a liberatory post-capitalist horizon predicated on
sharing limits, *Work, Want, Work* is a marvellously com-
pact, well-written, informative and thoughtful book.'

Sophie Lewis, author of *Full Surrogacy Now:*
*Feminism against Family*

# WORK
# WANT
# WORK

# About the authors

Mareile Pfannebecker is a writer and translator based in Manchester. She has published on Shakespeare, Renaissance travel writing, and critical theory.

J.A. Smith is the author of *Other People's Politics* and *Samuel Richardson and the Theory of Tragedy*. He is a lecturer in the English department at Royal Holloway, University of London.

# WORK
# WANT
# WORK

Labour and desire at the
end of capitalism

## MAREILE PFANNEBECKER AND J.A. SMITH

**ZED**

*Work Want Work: Labour and Desire at the End of Capitalism* was first published in 2020 by Zed Books Ltd, The Foundry, 17 Oval Way, London SE11 5RR, UK.

www.zedbooks.net

Typeset in Galliard and Garamond by Swales & Willis Ltd, Exeter, Devon
Cover design by Alice Marwick
Cover illustration © iStock/turk_stock_photographer

Printed and bound by CPI Group (UK) Ltd, Croydon, CR0 4YY

A catalogue record for this book is available from the British Library

ISBN 978-1-78699-727-2 hb
ISBN 978-1-78699-728-9 pb
ISBN 978-1-78699-729-6 pdf
ISBN 978-1-78699-996-2 epub
ISBN 978-1-78699-730-2 mobi

Dedicated to the hundreds of thousands of activists who were politicised between 2015 and 2019, and fought to try and end the painful developments we describe in this book.

# Contents

# Preface: the putting to work of everything we do

This is the new *lifework* regime in the West, where all you do is work, and everything you do can be put to work. When you're working for money, more of *you* is being monetised, in more ways, and better, than ever before. They've got you on your breaks, they've got you in the bathroom, they've got your smiles, your wit, your 'working independently but thriving as part of a team', and they've got your well-being. You're doing stuff that's outside your remit, job description, and training, and you're doing stuff it used to be other colleagues' job to do. If you're unemployed, you still get put to work, and someone else is still going to make money out of it. After work, it's 'shadow work', and that used to be someone else's job and livelihood too. You're typing in train ticket details, scanning barcodes, bagging groceries. It doesn't matter what job you tell people you do. Everyone's a shop assistant, a train conductor, a waiter, a travel agent (if you're lucky ...), and a bank manager. Now you're home and you're still getting those work emails, or if you drive for Uber, ride for Deliveroo, or cam on Snapchat, you're still getting those jobs in. Even if no one will work all twenty-four hours of the day, for the first time in history, 'no moment, place, or situation now exists in which one *can not*'.[1]

Your fun looks like work too. Your social media is a continuously rolling modelling portfolio, show-reel, and curriculum vitae (even when a bad post gets you fired); and video games focus less on fighting and shooting, than on simulating managerial labour. Meanwhile it's the platform's owners who derive value from the labour of your laziness, your boredom, your desire, your anger, your trauma. And if none of this applies to you, if you work illegally, if you can't work, or try to say, 'I would prefer not to', you might just disappear.

Theodor Adorno wrote at the end of the 1960s of the perniciousness of the concept of 'free time', contrasting it with his own ideal of a scholarly life of unalienated labour, in which 'there is no hard and fast opposition between my work itself and what I do apart from it'.[2] The growing industry for organised leisure was a con, obscuring the reasonableness of the philosopher's demand that work itself should be pleasant and interesting: not something we feel constantly compelled to distance our 'true selves' from, eager to escape at the end of the day. Ironically, it was *life-work* that answered Adorno's call. There's no 'hard and fast opposition' between work and non-work now either, and your 'true self' is not only welcome at the workplace – whether it's Pret or JPMorgan Chase – in the emotional and affective labour we are all expected to perform, your 'true self' *has* to be there.

This book examines together several much-debated changes in work since Adorno's time to show that they are importantly interconnected. It claims that what we call the *lifework* regime has imposed on the West the following related ruptures. In Chapter 1, 'the tragedy of not being a baker' – the lost permanence and growing interchangeability between the tasks carried out in all kinds of traditional jobs and professions. In Chapter 2, a new porousness between the lives of the unemployed and those in low-pay employment we call *malemployment*, as well as new powers for the state to expel people from the economy and polity altogether, in a condition we call *disemployment*. And in Chapter 3, a 'Young-Girlification', where a quasi-adolescent self-commodification increasingly defines all other forms of work-based subjectivity.

We hope there is political potential simply in rec-ognising these processes as interconnected, but we also examine over the course of this book five existing attempts to respond to the problem of work. In the politics of the post-2016 'populist' moment, politicians of the right and left are invoking the era of the New Deal and post-war consensus as a time of stable employment, the policies of which could save us from the problems described above. Young radicals and anti-work activists make the apparently opposite demand for a hyper-technologised 'post-work' future; while an under-examined tradition of continental philosophy has resorted to art and literature to show the lengths one would have to go to imagine a kind of community that is not organised around work. In Chapter 4, we examine the alleged 'post-work' programme of Silicon Valley, with its model of extracting value, not from conscious labour, but from unconscious – and often destructive – kinds of desire in the form of data. We contrast this with a new wave of cultural criticism appearing in the late 2010s, which has in common the surreptitious demand that we 'repurpose our desire': to take the desires that have been so put to work by digital capitalism and redirect them as a means of breaking the *lifework* regime.

# 1

# Lifework

A conversation is staged over three decades in the work of Alexandre Kojève, Georges Bataille, Maurice Blanchot, Michel Foucault, Jean-Luc Nancy, and Giorgio Agamben, around these thinkers' shared and often conflicting use of the term *désœuvrement*: literally 'unworking', but also 'inoperability', 'the absence of work', and 'the absence of *a* work'. Less frequently taken up in scholarship on work than the vocabulary of work's three 'classical' inter-rogators, Karl Marx, Émile Durkheim, and Max Weber, the term's usefulness to the theory of work is in recog-nising *not-working* as something more than just a passive withdrawal of effort.[1] Instead, *not-working* is conceptual-ised as an active, positive, even material quality, and – as we conceive it – one that is increasingly under threat in the *lifework* regime. As every Humanities undergraduate eventually finds out, Foucault's early book, the *History of*

*Madness* (1961) argued that whereas previous periods in Europe's history had thought there was some oblique and mystified wisdom in mental illness, the seventeenth and eighteenth centuries subjected it to a 'great confinement', applying for the first time a rigorous medical taxonomy – with attendant forced hospitalisations – to the mad. Yet the era's authorities were not strict about separating this newly medicalised idea of madness from the confinement of paupers, beggars, and sexual delinquents: all those, in short, it regarded as socially useless because of their inability to work. In this way, Foucault says, 'madness was seen through an ethical condemnation of idleness in the social immanence now grounded on a community of work'.[2]

Historians of medicine sceptical of Foucault's remarkable association of madness and *désœuvrement* might well be right to question how 'prominent in eighteenth-century discourse the couplings Foucault emphasizes between sanity and work, madness and sloth' really were.[3] But to respond to Foucault's argument only on this empirical level of historical fact is to overlook part of the playful, philosophical, even literary logic of Foucault's own text. For what he later referred to as 'a phrase I ventured rather blindly: "madness, the absence of an oeuvre"', imposes itself in Foucault's *History* not only as a historical claim about how madness was excluded from a 'community of work' by a particular culture at a particular time. It also represents madness as oppositional to *a* work, in the sense meant when we refer to a 'work of art'. Foucault writes of a tradition of modern artists of madness – Sade, Goya, Hölderlin, Nerval, Nietzsche, Van Gogh, Artaud – whose creations represent 'precisely the *absence of an oeuvre*, the constantly repeated presence of that absence, the central void that is experienced and measured in its never-ending dimensions'.[4] When Foucault described a particular historical deployment of the idea of work – of labour – in an earlier epoch's treatment of madness, he did so with one eye on the existence of such a literature, which with every sentence, seems to try to undo the possibility of its totalisation and elevation as 'work', a concluded, canonical achievement.

To identify something called *désœuvrement* hiding in literature is to claim that the problem with 'great works' is precisely that they too readily get 'put to work': get treated as useful, improving, educational, or otherwise as status symbols, reaffirming hierarchies. And yet they nonetheless contain a certain 'mad' counter-flow that seeks to undermine the process altogether. The re-echoing voice in Foucault here is that of his sometime friend, Blanchot. In *The Space of Literature* (1955), Blanchot had expanded on an idea established at least since the 'art for art's sake' movement of the late nineteenth century: the bohemian doctrine that art is opposed to work because radically useless, free from all utilitarian responsibility of being morally or socially productive. Blanchot's upgraded version of this idea finds a rather gnomic parable in one of the important myths of the origin of art: that of Orpheus, doomed to sing forever of his love, Eurydice, whom he could have saved

3

from the Underworld had he only resisted the temptation to turn back and check she was still walking behind him. In Blanchot's retelling, Eurydice is art (the gender implications are not explored), 'the furthest art can reach', and is to be brought 'back to the light of day', given 'form, shape, and reality', by the task of the journey from the Underworld it falls to Orpheus to guide, as the work of the artist.

But before Eurydice the work of art can emerge into the light, Orpheus fecklessly abandons his task, unable to resist the temptation to look back at her too soon. Far from regarding this as a moralistic warning, however, Blanchot goes as far as to interpret the failure of Orpheus the worker as, in itself, the entire 'proper movement' of art. True art refuses its own manifesting as 'work'. In the analogy, Orpheus looks back not merely to Eurydice, still occluded in the night, but to 'what night hides, the *other* night': Orpheus shows himself an artist by wanting to see the unending dark, to see his own not-seeing as Eurydice turns away, and his subsequent fate, to sing an unending song of this dark, is in that sense the reward for his refusal of the work of the light of day.[5] It is tempting to say that the turning away of Eurydice under the gaze of Orpheus anticipates art withdrawing from its onlooker the instant it is perceived. Art, in this way, is not merely opposed to, but is always breaking with its own status as 'work'.

All this will seem a considerable distance from our discussions of low pay, precarity, and digital labour elsewhere in this book. As we show a little later in this chapter, it would take Nancy's development of the idea of *désœuvrement* to reveal its full social application. But at its simplest, when we say that work is coming to characterise more and more parts of ours lives, what we mean is that it is this space of *désœuvrement* – that which is opposed to and undoes work – that is facing a greater and greater diminishment. So much so, that it is becoming increasingly difficult to make these thinkers' imaginative leap to 'something that is not work'.

## On not being a baker

In 1998, the sociologist Richard Sennett wrote of returning to a large bakery in Boston, whose workers he had first met and interviewed twenty-five years earlier. Previously, Sennett had observed a homogeneously Greek immigrant workforce, tied together by a combination of the local union and family. The bakers did not enjoy their work – it was often extremely arduous and the hours were antisocial – but it was also highly specialised and technically difficult to perform, and the ability to do it well was valued among them. Revisiting the bakery in the 1990s, Sennett found that the work of the Greek bakers was now carried out by a non-unionised and ethnically mixed group of 'flexi-workers', operating extremely simple and user-friendly modern ovens. The dough no longer required muscle to pound, burning one's hands and arms while using the ovens was less likely, the different kinds of bread no longer required years of experience to be able to get right, and the old night shifts had been replaced with flexible part-time schedules, now filled by both women and men.[6]

As Sennett suggests, what is remarkable about the second group of workers is that it is impossible for them to think of themselves as bakers, or even as particularly or permanently attached to the baking industry. The characteristic actions of their work could just as well be performed in any number of other areas of the service sector. At the time of Sennett's first visit in the early 1970s, it was becoming common to speak of a 'knowledge economy' to come, where cognitive skills would replace manual labour.[7] Yet the second visit demonstrates how technological advances welcomed for making labour more 'cognitive' in this way can also have the opposite effect: flattening out tasks that once required extremely specialised knowledge, and replacing them with work that could not be less edifying. 'In all forms of work, from sculpting to serving meals, people identify with tasks which challenge them, tasks which are difficult', Sennett concludes, 'by a terrible paradox, when we diminish difficulty and resistance, we create the very conditions for uncritical and indifferent activity on the part of the users'.[8]

If – as this book argues – we are living through a generalised diminishing of *désœuvrement* – the becoming-work-like of things that weren't work before – then one of the ironies is that it is taking place precisely alongside the dismantling of labour's conventional locus: the profession or career. In previous technological revolutions, while blue-collar labour was turned inside out, the middle-class professions retained their integrity, even cementing their position by representing themselves as the crucial overseers of new social realities. As a growing branch of scholarship claims, what is distinctive about the technological transformations of the turn of the twenty-first century is that the white-collar work of 'professionals', protected in previous eras, is now subject to a rapid automation of tasks, accompanied by precarity or deskilling for those who used to carry them out. In fact, as exponential developments in automation take place, it may be these kinds of white-collar workers who experience Sennett's 'tragedy of not being a baker' soonest.[9]

The examples of work's new colonisations of various parts of life that we describe in this book are occurring, then, in the context of a kind of capitalism that constitutes an immediate threat to the existence of much of its traditionally hegemonic class: 'the bourgeoisie', in which cultural capital and economic capital (the right to determine what is best in the culture and the ownership of property) historically coincide. This class looks back at an immediate past in which its cultural identity has been abandoned, a present where its traditional social and professional privileges have eroded, and a future that has no need of it at all. To take these three 'deaths' in turn: excepting some 'provincial cities of Europe, and perhaps ... certain regions of North America', the Marxist historian Perry Anderson has observed:

> [T]he bourgeoisie as Baudelaire or Marx, Ibsen or Rimbaud, Grosz or Brecht – or even Sartre or O'Hara – knew it, is a thing of the past. In place of that solid amphitheatre is an aquarium of floating, evanescent forms – the projectors and managers, auditors and janitors, administrators and speculators of contemporary capital: functions of a monetary universe that knows no social fixities or stable identities.[10]

The bowler-hatted fathers of Wendy Darling and of Mary Poppins's charges provided both the shocked denouncers and the main audience for the century of avant-garde culture Anderson invokes, before negotiating their surrender to mass culture in the decades following the Second World War. 'As capitalism brought a relative well-being to the lives of large working masses in the West', writes Franco Moretti of this post-war moment, 'commodities became the new principle of legitimation: consensus was built on things, not men – let alone principles. It was the dawn of today: capitalism triumphant, and bourgeois culture dead'.[11]

This surrender of the bourgeoisie's unique claim to 'culture' preceded the dismantling of its mode of work: the trading of Anderson's 'amphitheatre' of exclusive professional expertise for the 'aquarium' of continuously floating functions, tasks, and roles. As Richard and Daniel Susskind describe, the late twentieth and early twenty-first centuries have seen technological challenge to the gatekeeping expertise of bourgeois professionals in health, education, divinity, law, journalism, management, tax and auditing, and architecture, democratising their knowledge, distributing their tasks across several less-elevated workers, and – in some cases – automating their roles altogether.[12] If Sennett recognised the tragedy of not being a baker, it is also possible today to be, *but not exactly be* a teacher, a lecturer, a solicitor, or an architect either, as these professionals complain that more and more of what they used to do *uniquely* is crowded out by interchangeable bureaucratic tasks and 'customer facing' affective labour.

'Employees are increasingly entreated to take on tasks that their occupation previously did not require – teachers are engaged in health promotion activities, university lecturers are encouraged to ensure the employability of their graduates, and doctors are called upon to advise on healthy life styles rather than specifically treating illnesses', observe Peter Fairbrother and Gavin Poynter.[13] Interviews with academic librarians shown to us by Penny Andrews evidenced these workers' irritation at being expected to take more and more compliance tasks (ensuring academics comply with fast-changing rules about how their research is made available to the public) in addition to those they recognised as proper to librarianship itself. Such professions increasingly resemble the extreme form of Anderson's 'aquarium', referred to by David Graeber as 'bullshit jobs': jobs made up of interchangeable flows of managerial, clerical, sales and service tasks, which often seem to exist only to create time-filling bureaucratic tasks for each other to perform.[14] If this can be seen as the record of the scattering of a hegemonic class, it is also – in Michael Hardt and Antonio Negri's terms – a change in the hegemonic form of labour: the kind of labour, that is, which 'impose[s] ... a tendency on other forms of labour and society itself', so that everything gets gradually reconstructed in its image.[15] Bullshit jobs are what happens when it doesn't matter which job you applied for; they are all subject to the same rules of customer service increasingly encumbered by routine administration.

These processes are reflected in the logic of the professional networking app LinkedIn, which breaks down the experience on one's CV into a series of isolatable 'skills', with colleagues and former employers invited to vouch for one's efficacy in each. On LinkedIn, one is less a lawyer or a land-surveyor, than a composition of separate abilities that might be appealing to any number of kinds of employer: a logic increasingly replicated in job application and interview processes, and extended to more and more parts of one's life history. 'Activities which were felt to be valuable in their own right are reframed in the language of employability', as David Frayne describes, 'my charity work with the homeless must be mentioned because it has given me experience in the voluntary sector, and my hitchhike across

Europe promoted because it has developed my ability to use initiative and solve problems'.[16]

Criticisms of these processes tend to be made from the point of view of the welfare of the worker, in the manner of Sennett's position that such erosions of clarity about what our work consists of are specifically psychologically damaging. But limiting our perspective in this way overlooks the broader authoritarian social drift that these work practices have lent themselves to. Since the 2014 Immigration Act, Britain has pursued a 'Hostile Environment' policy against illegal immigrants, which includes having landlords and employers check the immigration credentials of those they house or employ, but also obligates public sector workers to do the same while discharging their services. As of 2015, the latest extension of the UK's 'Prevent' anti-terrorism strategy has obligated teachers, council workers, social workers, doctors, university lecturers, nurses, librarians, and opticians to identify and refer anyone fitting the profile of 'vulnerable to terrorism'.[17] Andrews's librarians resented having a 'compliance' function imposed on their relations with the academics they work alongside. The same pattern is found in both these state policies, only here it is the most oppressive and illiberal tendencies of the state that are appearing in the gaps in our increasingly fragmented professional roles. These tendencies become 'embedded', as the campaign group Liberty have put it, 'in everyday interactions between trusted public sector workers and the people they are supposed to serve: nurses and patients, police and victims of crime and teachers and their pupils'.[18]

## Nostalgia for work

We have hardly addressed the kinds of precarious, low-paid jobs lower down the social scale that, in Chapter 2, we will describe as 'malemployment'. Nor have we touched on the variations on these processes and their human effects in the economy globally. Yet even within these limited parameters, the picture emerging from the changes in work we have discussed is dark. There is a risk, however, that in focusing on how the break-up of stable and clearly defined careers has numerous negative effects on workers and invites reactionary political deployments of work, one ends up implicitly idealising an older model of work. The danger, in other words, is in imagining that all our problems could be solved if only we could push back on these changes, and return to something like the working model of the post-war era: to a time when wages were high and careers were lifelong, and we were not yet entangled in the tyranny of extraneous 'bullshit' that has built up in the fragmented workplace of the succeeding neoliberal decades.

The post-war period's achievement of peak economic equality and robust trade unionism makes it an appealing memory for today's left; even as this places it in what has been described as 'the paradoxical situation of having to defend ... institutions that we criticised earlier for not being radical enough'.[19] It is no coincidence that Bernie Sanders invokes the legacy of Franklin Roosevelt, while socialists on both sides of the Atlantic have tried to make radical environmental reform palatable with the branding of a 'Green New Deal'. It is even tempting to think of the unlikely emergence of Sanders and Jeremy Corbyn as figureheads for the young left as partly attributable to their being old enough to have been political agents (albeit of a minor kind) in this pre-neoliberal world. On the right, a parallel nostalgia underlies Donald Trump's talk of 'bringing back jobs' to the immiserated Rust Belt, and the Brexit Leave campaign's message of freeing Britain from the 'red tape' of Brussels bureaucrats and from immigrants 'taking our jobs'. Both left and right, in other words, have a 'nostalgia for work', arranged – openly or not – around the norms of the post-war settlement.[20] And this nostalgia involves acting as if the shortcomings, forms of precariousness and everyday violence that existed in that earlier settlement were merely local flaws.

The working world of the post-war regime was born of the economic trauma of the Great Depression, the demands of working-class movements that promises of a better society made during the Second World War be honoured, and the threat of actually-existing communism to the East if they weren't. Its aspiration was that a generous welfare state should create basic entitlements beyond waged work, while being contingent on most people performing it; a rooting premise that Andrea Komlosy refers to as the 'inevitable, quasi-automatic connection between proletarianization and social protection'.[21] 'Automatic' as it came to seem, the possibility of this connection between waged work and social protection was in fact strikingly novel, beginning only with the Bismarck Chancellorship in Germany, the Liberal reforms of 1909 in Britain, and the 1930s New Deal in the USA. As Robert Castel has argued, it represented nothing short of a reversal of the association the pre-industrial world had made between waged work and vulnerability, which had held that it was those who 'slipped down' from independent artisanship into dependent labour who were the precarious ones.[22]

The post-war regime's grounding in this recently formed 'connection' led it to two potentially deleterious gestures. First, it had the effect of further *universalising* work. Post-war welfare states took responsibility for protecting those out of work and hoped to render certain areas of life (health, education, old age) universally non-contingent on it. Yet these processes constituted, in Guy Standing's terms, only a 'fictitious decommodification'. '"Universalistic" meant covering the needs of formal employees':[23] to treat those out of work fully 'as free citizens' was regarded as 'inconsistent with the principles of a free community'.[24] Even as they offered new protection to those out of work, welfare regimes naturalised the idea that truly belonging to their citizenry meant being in waged work. Second, the structure of the post-war work regime had the effect of *essentialising* work and what counted as work. The male waged worker was its standard unit, supported in the domestic sphere by a housewife whose domestic work (rarely recognised as such) was subsidiary to her new role as chief consumer of the Keynesian-Fordist economy's bounty, paid for by the new expectation of a 'family wage' for the male breadwinner. As Nancy Fraser points out, this also had the effect of 'institutionalising androcentric understandings of family and work' while 'naturaliz[ing] heteronormativity and gender hierarchy'.[25]

Even putting aside the ways such 'protection' of the family remained an at best mixed benefit to the women it ensconced, radicals of the time identified how its provision was still racialised and regional, and quickly collapsed when combined with other forms of injustice. Mariarosa Dalla Costa wrote in 1972 of the hypocrisy of post-war welfare states' claim to protect the nuclear family, when, in the regime's very heartlands, 'six-year-olds have already come up against police dogs in the South of the United States', and 'today we find the same phenomenon in Southern Italy and Northern Ireland'.[26] Angela Davis exposed how liberal policy-makers had absolved themselves of extending proper protections to black families, precisely (and ironically) with the self-accusation that slavery had done permanent damage to 'black masculinity' and so state protections for black families were bound to fail.[27] And in the psychoanalytic work of Shulamith Firestone, the ideal of the nuclear family was itself found to be sustained on exploited domestic labour from the 'black ghetto Whorehouse' (in the form of sex work, domestic work, and precarious menial labour, 'the black community in America makes possible the existence of the family structure of the larger white community'), creating new and pathological forms of racist fantasy on all sides in the process.[28]

Racialised inequality in general was also perpetuated, not as a by-product, but as a deliberate aim of essentialising definitions of work. Scholars such as Jill Quadagno and Ira Katznelson have shown how waves of progressive legislation remembered as having radically expanded social protection in post-war America, disproportionately excluded black Americans. This was the consequence of explicit compromises Roosevelt had made with Southern Democrats in the original striking of the New Deal. The main mechanism deployed to effect this exclusion was to fix benefits precisely to what we have seen was an 'essentialised' definition of waged work, which now excluded sharecroppers – the many Southerners who lived by borrowing equipment and farming materials from their landlords and paying off their debts at the end of the year – as well as domestic workers and day labourers: all work done disproportionately by black people. Continuing this pattern after the war, the majority of black Americans were not entitled to social security until the 1950s, unionisation was clamped down on in the South where most black people lived, and agricultural and domestic employers of primarily black workers were spared the requirement of a minimum wage and maximum hours.[29]

It is therefore not enough to claim that the post-war work regime was admirable in itself, but made insufficient allowances for women and non-whites. In both cases, these were not unfortunate slips, but the specific outcome of the definition of work at its very core: and the relegation within that definition of raced and gendered domestic and agricultural work. For the same reason, it is also not enough now, from the position of the new precarious work regime, to simply bewail the breaking of the 'inevitable connection' this earlier period made between waged work and social protection, as if retaining that bond would resolve the problem of precarity. As Isabel Lorey has pointed out, to frame matters in this way is to fall to too ready an opposition between 'security', 'stability', 'normality' on the one hand, and 'precarity' on the other. That is, to fail to consider either 'who was already not (sufficiently) safeguarded in the Fordist welfare-state system', or 'in what way social insecurity is currently becoming a component of social reality': that is, a grim kind of stable norm in itself.[30] The many ways in which the latter is the case we will consider in the following chapter. To conclude the discussion of nostalgia for work: criticising today's precarious work landscape carries with it the danger of inadvertently idealising the previous one. This is troublesome because a regime, which for all its welcome protections of parts of life *outside* work for some, was nonetheless constructed around a damagingly essentialising and universalising definition *of* work as such that, like all universalisms, effectively concealed the many that it left out.

## What will we do in the post-work utopia?

For all that, it still seems remarkable how convinced post-war culture apparently was that part of its destiny was that the amount of time we spend in work would inevitably be subject to a massive reduction. In a text written in the depths of the Great Depression in 1930, 'Economic Possibilities for our Grandchildren', John Maynard Keynes – the economist who would posthumously become the guiding voice of post-war economies – had treated the arrival of a fifteen-hour working week and luxury for all as virtually inevitable. His analysis set the horizon of such post-war investigations of the nature of economic growth as Anthony Crosland's *The Future of Socialism* (1956) and J.K. Galbraith's *The Affluent Society* (1958).[31] As the confidence of this liberal tradition subsided with the crisis of the economic model that sustained it, the reduction of work returned to being a priority of the left. During 1968, Raoul Vaneigem condemned not only capitalism but also Soviet and Maoist communism for their collusion in the universalisation of the principle of work.[32] In Italy, a hippie-inflected Marxist movement demanded 'zero work for income' and proclaimed, '*the revolution is probable*'.[33] And in Britain, as the Edward Heath government responded to fuel shortages and industrial action by imposing a three-day working week, many were surprised at the creativity and experimentalism the partial liberation from work brought out in them.[34]

As ideologically heterogeneous as these positions were, it is startling to realise that their shared assumption was the desirability and probability – if not the inevitability – that a version of Keynes's luxury post-work future would come to pass. Not only this, as Peter Frase puts it, people 'actually worried about what people would do after being liberated from work'.[35] In the 1950s and 1960s, there was even a significant minor industry of liberal cultural criticism committed to anticipating the *dangers* human sensibility would face if it was liberated into the free play of consumption in the affluence to come.[36] So far from such a starting point today, says Frayne, 'we would be forgiven for seeing earlier predictions for a radically reduced working week as nothing more than a historical curio – a nice but rather outlandish idea that was forgotten decades ago'.[37] But efforts are being made to reverse this great forgetting. The most radical of these are found among the 'anti-work' movement of thinkers and activists who demand that the new conditions of work described above be seized by the left: not in the spirit of 'nostalgia for work', but to demand a 'postcapitalist', 'post-work' society, sustained by 'full automation'.

The argument, put briefly, is that current developments in digital technology are placing capitalism in the position of being able to absorb less and less labour, while production itself becomes easier and easier. At the same time, 'value' is increasingly found not in objects and their labour time, but in rents collected on intellectual property, with the effect of creating an unsustainable degree of monopoly ownership. In the face of dystopian predictions of mass unemployment, anti-work thinkers propose to simply go with the grain of these changes, to take capital at its word about the superfluity of labour, and to demand the transition to a post-work society. As much work as possible could be performed by machines, with humans left to pursue flourishing in all the areas of life they are currently kept from by bullshit work, sustained – for as long as money is an appropriate unit of exchange – by something like a Universal Basic Income (UBI), paid to all citizens.

Our stress here is not on the empirical limits of technology, the political challenge of transitioning to such societies in the context of global inequality, or the environmental implications.[38] Nor do we respond to the justified misgivings of some campaigners, who point out that the UBI idea originated with neoliberal thinkers who wanted to use it as an excuse for abandoning targeted welfare altogether, or who see it as an economically false concession that mass unemployment is inevitable, rather than a result of political choices.[39] Our interest here and once again in Chapter 4 is rather in the philosophical implications of the 'post-work hypothesis';[40] both in terms of what such tools of analysis can tell about what a society commensurate with the theory of *désœuvrement* could look like, and also what it means that – now – at the very moment of 'lifework' and the 'putting to work of everything we do', this formerly unfashionable fantasy should have returned to our collective imaginary and to our radical politics.

Much of Frayne's *The Refusal of Work* (2015) is given to a series of case studies of people in Britain who have tried to escape their hectic and unhappy work lives by doing as little paid work as possible. A common perception among them is that one of the main impediments in such attempts to anticipate a 'post-work' life is the moral judgement and exclusion they experience in a society where so much sociability and sense of worth is organised around work. That said, Frayne warns, 'a lot of popular anti-capitalist polemic' also 'tells people (often in a rather pious fashion) that they will be happier if they choose to work less and moderate their spending'.[41] As much as the 'work ethic' is obviously moralised in culture, it seems there is also the danger of an equivalent moralism of the refusal to participate in capitalist culture, meaning that work and non-work both end up being justified in moralising terms. Frayne tries to avoid this trap by declining to romanticise his subjects' struggles, and by emphasising how hard it is in our current culture for ordinary people to try to work less. However, when he does become specific about what people could be doing if they were not working, he steps into what we argue is one of the main inbuilt dangers of anti-work writing as a genre: the speed with which naming something as a *possibility* for the good life we could pursue, if freed from work, turns into a *prescription* about what it is we should be doing. As one of the most prolific anti-work writers, André Gorz has remarked, 'it is the function of utopias ... to provide us with the distance from the existing state of affairs which allows us to judge what we are doing in the light of what we *could* or *should* do'.[42] The separation between the '*could*' and the '*should*', we argue, is not so easy to police.

Several of Frayne's interviewees found that giving up work in fact gave them a head-start on making up for lost income because they were no longer paying for the many services they only needed because they were spending so much time in work. 'Given the extent to which many modern commodities – from pre-prepared meals to high-caffeine drinks, car washes, repair services, care services, personal trainers, dating agencies and so on – are capitalising on our lack of free-time', Frayne says, 'it is not surprising that many of the people I met found that working less was allowing them to save money. They were able to do more for themselves'.[43] Perhaps doing one's own chores and looking after one's children or relatives *is* better than many people's paid work. The problem, we suggest, comes in at the point that much anti-work discourse ends up having to assume it is *necessarily* better. Wherever one comes down on the question, this *is* a kind of moral evaluation and implicit prescriptiveness, and it means that Frayne's discourse, like that of many others making a similar case, cannot avoid a certain structural 'piety' of the kind he imputes to both mainstream pro-work opinion and anti-capitalist activism.

Not only this, but the move also risks repeating the core gesture of the industrial and post-war work regimes:

of essentialising paid 'labour' as qualitatively different from domestic and social-reproductive 'work' (in Chapter 3, we will turn to the major tradition of feminism that has made the case that it is a kind of labour for capitalism in itself). One can only sign up to the idea that doing these things 'for ourselves' is necessarily liberating if one agrees that waged work is the only thing that makes an arduous activity undesirable. The implication of such an ideology is that child-rearing, cooking, even sex, are all an unalienated good ... until you get paid for them, at which point they're instantaneously transfigured into 'bad' labour.

Something more of the logic behind 'doing more for ourselves' can be understood by returning to one of the canonical versions of the argument that liberation from certain kinds of work can give rise to personal autonomy and creativity. 'Daughters of educated men have always done their thinking from hand to mouth', ran Virginia Woolf's famous defence of female creativity stifled under patriarchy, 'they have thought while they stirred the pot, while they rocked the cradle'.[44] It would be tempting to see Woolf's demand for autonomy from drudgery as one of the prototypes for today's anti-work movement. But on closer inspection, Frayne's comments turn out to have more in common with those of Woolf's harshest detractors. 'I feel bound to disagree with Mrs. Woolf's assumption that running a household and family unaided necessarily hinders or weakens thinking', remarked Q.D. Leavis in a review of Woolf's *Three Guineas* (1938) in the literary journal *Scrutiny*, 'one's own kitchen and nursery, and not the drawing-room and dinner-table ... is the realm where living takes place, and I see no profit in letting our servants live for us'.[45] This objection is inflected by class, contrasting Leavis's (and *Scrutiny*'s) petit-bourgeois self-reliance to Woolf's suspiciously louche 'drawing-room' bohemianism. In one of the better jokes in literary criticism, Leavis wonders whether someone of Woolf's background would 'know which end of the cradle to stir'.

For Leavis, intellectual creation and self-fulfilment are not to be abstracted from the tasks of ordinary life, but draw their strength precisely from them: though in Leavis's case this comes at the cost of her silence over whether men are expected to find the cradle-stirring intellectually rewarding too.[46] No more inclined than Leavis to 'let servants live our lives for us', Frayne refers to 'the injustice in a society where one section of the population buys their free-time by offloading their chores on to the other'.[47] But – as for Leavis – it is not merely unjust that many of us offload our unpleasant but regrettably necessary day-to-day tasks: rather, *we* are also missing out when our hectic work lives oblige us to do so. We were duped into thinking work was life, and now we learn that life is staying at home.

This is not to accuse Frayne of some special theoretical neglect. It is simply a problem structural to anti-work writing. While the post-work hypothesis aims to rescue us from both the material need and the faulty moralism that keeps us in jobs we hate, it does so by proposing a better life 'after work'. What will make it better it falls to the anti-work writer to define; and it is very difficult to make such a definition without becoming surreptitiously prescriptive. This problem surfaces whenever anti-work writing is forced to become specific about what everyone is projected to do once they have stopped working for a wage, even beyond the simple example of domestic and social-reproductive work we have focused on thus far. For instance, the futures envisaged by other recent anti-work authors such as Frase, Nick Srnicek and Alex Williams, Helen Hester, and Sophie Lewis, all avoid idealising caring and social-reproductive activities by returning to the old demand of Second-Wave feminists such as Firestone that 'full automation' should extend to these forms of work too.[48] Much 'highly personal and embarrassing care work … might be better carried out by robots', they argue, while even 'the pain and suffering involved in pregnancy [c]ould be relegated to the past, rather than mystified as natural and beautiful'.[49] Yet this only pushes the question a frame back. If we are not (primarily) caring for babies and the elderly, then what are we doing?

The totemic example of this bind can be found in Marx himself. In a remark in *The German Ideology*, which every anti-work writer must quote sooner or later, Marx proposes that under ideal circumstances, communism would make it possible 'to hunt in the morning, fish in the afternoon, rear cattle in the evening, criticize after dinner, just as I have a mind'.[50] As we will see in Chapter 4, Marx is not naïve to the dangers of trying to determine what people are to do with their new freedom; and some anti-work writers have followed him in this reservation, declining to make predictions and to instead focus on demands.[51] Yet there are enough statements of this kind across Marx's writings for his more humanist admirers to see him as the philosopher of a kind of personal liberation, the core values of which do indeed seem to have been set in advance:

> Marx, the man who every year read all the works of Aeschylus and Shakespeare, who brought to life in himself the greatest works of human thought, would never have dreamt that his idea of socialism could be interpreted as having as its aim [merely] the well-fed and well-clad 'welfare' or 'workers' state. Man, in Marx's view, has created in the course of history a culture which he will be free to make his own when he is freed from the chains, not only of economic poverty, but of the spiritual poverty created by alienation.[52]

It is not incidental that these examples of fulfilling human activity – from fishing to reading Aeschylus – are made up entirely of what we might call 'productive enjoyments'. It is not about viewing waxworks and magic lanterns in the morning, reading penny novels in the afternoon, and drinking gin all evening (all of which must doubtless be left behind as the pastimes of alienated 'spiritual poverty'). Though they are aware of the problem (as we show in Chapter 4), the analogous statements in Srnicek and Williams are similarly compelled to reassure us of their 'productiveness': 'leisure should not be confused with idleness, as many things we enjoy most involve immense amounts of effort. Learning a musical instrument, reading literature, socializing with friends and playing sports all involve varying degrees of effort'.[53] And so in Frayne: 'shorter working hours would open up more space for political engagement, for cultural creation and appreciation, and for the development of a range of voluntary and self-defined activities outside work'.[54]

Comparing the post-work utopias envisaged by two of Marx's immediate successors, William Morris and Oscar Wilde, Owen Hatherley points out that 'while Morris imagines everyone becoming village craftsmen, Wilde imagines them all becoming leisured polymaths'.[55] What they share, however, is the archetypal anti-work rhetorical dependence on making the case that, not only should we do away with work because it is unjust, unnecessary, and damaging, but also because the alternative activities we would be freed to do would be indisputably good for us. But there will be some for whom even the new leisure activities themselves – be they Morris's handicrafts, Wilde's new Renaissance of art, or Marx's Aeschylus – would be encountered as a totally alienating set of tasks in themselves. We consider in Chapter 4 the anti-work writers who are attempting the opposite move of abolishing work while having no aspiration to prescribe the 'cultural' lives of those it is liberating (as well as the problems that come with that approach too). For now, we note that our aim is not to dismiss out of hand the content of various visions of the good life; no doubt many will find the activities proposed by the anti-work writers discussed above appealing. The point is rather that the 'good' is aimed at according to an uninspected set of moral and cultural imperatives. As such, post-work visions run the danger of conceding to a humanism that doesn't respect that we cannot know what the other wants, and does not take seriously the idea that a consensus on the basis of a life well spent, if there may be such a thing, is liable to change.

## Literary communism

Work always points beyond itself, socially, culturally, and politically. For the thinkers of *désœuvrement* introduced in this chapter's first section, the concept as well as the material experience of 'work' shapes the ways in which we think about ourselves; Nancy in particular, in *The Inoperative Community* (1991), describes the ways in which work structures ideas of human community in different political models. Communism is Nancy's most obvious example. For Nancy, communism is fundamentally based on the ideal of a community of human beings defined as 'producers, and fundamentally as the producers of their own essence in the form of their labour or their work'.[56] You are what you do;

or rather, what you do simultaneously describes the human club and proves your membership in it.

Nancy argues that work, in the context of community, always does such ideological overtime, whether in Soviet communism, Nazi fascism, or the neoliberal regimes of the 1980s that provide Nancy's own context. William Empson made a similar observation in his discussion of government propaganda relating to the lingering unemployment of the 1930s in *Versions of the Pastoral* (1935). One poster discussed by Empson shows a worker with a chisel and reassuring statistics of 'men back at work': 'to accept the picture is to feel that the skilled worker's interests are bound up with his place in the class system and the success in British foreign policy in finding markets'. On top of that, Empson adds, the talismanic image of the worker provokes the conviction in his compatriots that 'while he is like this he is Natural and that will induce Nature to make us prosperous'.[57] So what Empson calls the 'mythic' work in the poster encourages its 1930s viewer to content themselves with the current arrangements of labour and class, and to identify with the political status quo in the form of the government and the nation.

The problem with such talismanic deployments of work, as Nancy sees it, is that as a 'regulative idea' of community it has a structurally totalitarian bent, even in ostensibly non-totalitarian contexts. 'Economic ties, technological operations, and political fusions (into a *body* or under a *leader*)' all present themselves as the necessary realisation of the community's essence.[58] This, Nancy insists, is inevitably a bad thing, and leads to concentration camps, gulags, and refugee detention camps, as well as less visible forms of violence. Work is put to work to lend hard and unequivocal borders to a community. Immigration, instrumentalised by both left and right either as a threat to the job market or as a benefit to a given economy, is likely the most visible and most common fashion of this 'putting to work' of work in political discourse today; meanwhile, having a job lined up will commonly make the difference between a rejected and an accepted citizenship application. For Nancy, the question is whether it is even possible to envisage a form of non-coercive work, with an attendant kind of community that refuses essentialism and exclusivity. Nancy's own, surprising answer is that there is, and that a glimmer of it might be found to be 'communism's secret', for instance, in gestures of Marx of the kind discussed above, where a promise is held out for 'a reign of freedom, one beyond the collective regulation of necessity, in which surplus work would no longer be exploitative work, but rather art and invention'.[59] According to Nancy's reading of Marx, it would seem that the substantial amount of free time that post-work models of society promise to everyone might be just the thing required for a community to resist totalitarianism.

'Art and invention' must shoulder a heavy burden here – how could they have the power to undo the structurally conservative function of the ideal of work in a given community? We have already suggested that the kinds of creative activity anti-work writers tend to reach for when describing what we are to do in the post-work utopia end up containing their own 'work-like' prescriptiveness, inimical to *désœuvrement*. More generally, popular culture has been sceptical of the idea that 'creativity', however broadly defined, might successfully replace paid labour as a way of structuring life in any form of society. A deep-rooted suspicion, often instinctively called up as a response to post-work propositions like UBI, is that self-directed creativity must lead to infantilising laziness or chaos. Bourgeois nineteenth-century literature did its share to bolster this idea; in Charles Dickens's *Bleak House* (1853), amateur artist Harold Skimpole lives in an alternative world of unfinished sketches, half-composed airs, and sky-gazing with his many artistically inclined children and grandchildren, all precariously dependent on the charity of his wealthier friends. The novel leaves no room to doubt the wickedness of this arrangement. It emphasises not only Skimpole's exploitation of his benefactors but also insists that his childish refusal of paid labour is synonymous with a fundamental moral irresponsibility, which precipitates several of the novel's eventual tragedies. The artist and his family's refusal to work for money threatens to unravel the social fabric as it leads to exploit and ultimately to destroy others alongside the moral order by which they live.

That it is not parasitism alone that we have learnt to suspect in those on the side of art against work, but a more far-reaching affront to the idea of citizenship itself, might be demonstrated in the prevalent hostile reaction to those who have erected their own communities in real life, within but apart from modern capitalism, with the goal of sharing labour in such a way that it creates as much time as possible for 'art and invention' for all of its members. Modern utopian socialist communes, as have existed at least since European socialists settled in nineteenth-century California, tend to be presented in media and fiction as cultish and fascistic at worst and, like Skimpole and his family, as deluded and naïve at best.[60] In one episode of the TV drama *Mad Men*, Roger Sterling, boss of the creative, dynamic, relatively underdog advertising firm, spends a day in 1970 on a hippie commune with his grown-up daughter, who has retreated there to escape from the strictures of bourgeois motherhood. He initially seems charmed by the commune's care-free ways where 'everyone does what they want', but among the pregnant, potato-peeling women gathered around a young man who apparently does little apart from owning a truck, Roger comes to the unspoken conclusion that the egalitarian ethics of the commune is a cover for a patriarchal order in miniature, and so tries and fails to import his daughter back to his own 'real' world as the lesser, more honest evil.

The consistent hostility of these tropes document the provocation represented by the proposal that self-directed creativity might replace work. The often passionate protests raised by the idea reveal the instinctive understanding, and fear, that changing the meaning of work must change the principles of politics, community, and human life alongside.

It is precisely this risk Nancy asks us to embrace when he suggests that the horizon of free time in Marx's writing promises room for 'art and invention' as a 'reign of freedom', as a route to a *désœuvrement* that would not only free us from unwanted work but also 'unwork' conventional ideas of the state, the self, and of labour.

To understand how, we need to turn to Nancy's philosophical ideas on 'being' itself. According to Nancy, what is at issue when a state, a self, or a product of our labour – like a work of art – is presented as 'perfectly detached, distinct and closed', this is a fundamental ontological error.[61] Neither workers nor nations nor 'works' are ever absolutely detached from the rest of the world. Nancy points out that we cannot even do as much as say 'I' in any meaningful way unless there are other 'I's, even if at moments the other 'I's are as minimal as voices in our heads. 'Solitude', Nancy points out, 'is a pretense': we are never truly alone, we can only be 'singular plural': it is the plurality of the more than one that makes the singular possible in the first instance.[62] This might serve to explain why in fiction, the idea of an isolated human, the only one left, is often raised but just as often breaks down. Where there is one, there are others of some form, and in their absence, scattered objects of human culture come starkly alive, like tins of food do in the scorched landscapes of Cormac McCarthy's *The Road* (2006), or the footprint, the human entrails left by cannibals, or the disembodied human voice imitated by a parrot in Daniel

Defoe's *Robinson Crusoe* (1719). To Nancy, this applies on the most basic, physical level – singular living bodies only exist and can only experience themselves as singular at the point of touch, at the limits that expose them to other bodies and other objects of resistance. 'Community means', Nancy concludes, 'that there is no singular being without another singular being, and that there is, therefore, an originary or ontological 'sociality'.[63] We never are alone – and we never work alone, either.

Nancy's view not only refuses the individual its self-contained independence, but also bars it from the option of transcendence of the self by communion with the larger entity of a group, even a group as generously defined as all of mankind or even all life on earth. These two rejected positions correlate with those occupied by Woolf and Q.D. Leavis discussed above. While 'a room of one's own' undeniably is a good material prerequisite for concentrated writing, it is also the emblem for a freedom from outside interruption that stands for just the kind of modern individualism that Woolf's Bloomsbury supported. As Raymond Williams suggests, the Bloomsbury group, so keen to point out that they were not really a group but merely a collection of individual artists and thinkers, were united in their variously artistic, political, and economic endeavours to ensure the autonomy and free expression of the 'civilised' individual without change to society overall.[64] While the door of Woolf's hypothetical room keeps out the housework that goes on below stairs, it also keeps at bay questions about the splendid isolation of the 'individual intelligence' that works within: the problem with making 'a room of one's own' your avatar for freedom is it is 'a room of *one's* own'. Q.D. Leavis's embrace of housework and childcare as manifestation of living your 'own' life, by contrast, assumes that the tedium of everyday tasks provides communion with the essence of the culture via the spirit of family.

In Nancy's version of community, by contrast, singular beings remain singular beings. Nancy's vision offers a way of looking at singularity and multiplicity at the same time, as 'being singular plural'. Nancy presents us with a world that does not have meaning as a unified whole but only has meaning at the demarcations that make and remake different, unique but not individual singularities: 'at every single instant singular beings share their limits, share each other on their limits'.[65] Nancy's 'being singular plural' would point not only to how the door makes Woolf and how the family laundry makes Leavis but to what other 'shared limits' are kept from view by the reification of each, and what cultures they work to support – that of upper middle-class individualism and the bourgeois family respectively.

Nancy's contextual, differential logic has much in common with the work of other poststructuralist thinkers and especially with that of his friend Jacques Derrida. Like Derrida, Nancy insists that meaning does not adhere to essences but is made at the demarcations of living beings as well as of objects and systems like language; to an extent, what Derrida calls *différance* and the trace, Nancy calls shared limits: it's the space between words that makes meaning as much as it is the 'between' between the 'you' and the 'I' that makes two mutually defining singularities. Both insist that in consequence of this logic of multiplying differences, a system of language, just like a group of living beings, is never complete or closed off against its multiple outsides.[66] Nancy's own version of these ideas stands out in its insistence that this differential logic is community itself, community understood as a form of communication: 'communication is the constitutive fact of an exposition to the outside that defines singularity'.[67] If that means we have nothing in common but (to communicate) our differences, to Nancy that is the opposite of nothing, as it is only the sharing of limits, or being-with, that delineates the existence of singular beings at a given moment.

The reason that all this amounts to *désœuvrement* is that being exposed at our limits to others leads to 'the risk – or the chance – of changing identity in it'.[68] For Nancy, 'art and literature' are not different from people in this respect; in fact, they are the privileged instance of 'being singular plural' and 'unworking' as the logic of life in general. Works of literature are evident instances of the exceptional and so of the singular, yet of a singularity that only exists inside a shared language; meanwhile its existence changes the contours of that very language and what is sayable and conceivable in it, which is also why there is no stepping outside those shared and multiplying limits at a future point.

It's what Derrida infamously refers to when he writes that 'there is no outside of the text'.[69] People as well as books lean into each other in order to exist in the first instance; a book's cover and human skin are foldable limits rather than absolute containers.

This then, would be literary communism; the acknowledgement that community is the risk, and the chance, of changing identity at multiplying limits with other people, objects and stories around us; but also, the active pursuit of encounters at these limits. Nancy sees hope on the side of Marx's endorsement of daily free time for 'art and invention' because here, art as we know it can become the place holder for a general freedom to experiment, not in empty space but in encounters with limits so significant they will warp your very shape. In as far as there is a vision of the future in this, it doesn't give away much detail; the difference to visions of 'free time' as individualist freedom or homely family pursuits is the enormous creative potential it bundles, where it imagines people sufficiently well fed and comfortable to pursue creative difference as a source of pleasure and creative self-modification. Literary communism's political significance lies in the link Nancy draws between community and work, and it is one that should arm us against the nostalgia for work discussed in this chapter. If work has the structuring function in a community in the way Nancy describes, then there are links between the kind of work that excludes many from its benefits and yet presents itself as freely available, and nations that declare themselves open to the world while building unyielding borders. Accordingly, an alternative form of work, one that is not the prize in a fight-to-the-death job market but a form of production based on creatively shared limits, might make forms of community more accepting of its changeable and multiple boundaries.

# 2

# Work expulsions

Lucian Freud painted Sue Tilley, a job centre employee, four times between 1994 and 1996. The most famous product of the relationship is 'The Benefits Supervisor Sleeping' (1995), now in the possession of Roman Abramovich. The large oil painting depicts the life-sized obese naked body of white, middle-aged, short-haired Tilley, asleep on a tattered sofa. The painting is difficult to interpret, its representation of Tilley ambivalent in both political and gender terms. It is part of what might be seen as the project of Freud's work, to reduce the human body to an un-idealised mass of flesh. That project culminated in the famous official portrait, 'HM Queen Elizabeth II' (2000–2001), in which the kitsch realism conventional in such patriotic exercises is supplanted by an unkindly masculinising fleshliness or meatiness of the sovereign's face. The equivalent subversion in 'The Benefits Supervisor Sleeping' is of the tradition of the idealised female nude. One thinks of the Velázquez 'Rokeby Venus', vandalised in the National Gallery by the suffragette Mary Richardson in 1914. In its refusal of the history of art's traditional idealising gaze, Freud's painting opens itself up to a feminist appropriation, perhaps even a celebration of the assertive presence of expansive human substance. But at the same time, the potential for misogyny in the painting is difficult to avoid. Misogyny's canonical writers – from Jonathan Swift to Martin Amis – refused to idealise female flesh too, and *surely* we are being invited to find Tilley disgusting. But the painting doesn't tell us to feel any such thing. If you're disgusted, that's on you. The painting is one of those artworks where the effect is derived not from its committing to a particular prejudice 'internally', as part of an aesthetic convention with established rules, but from wagering that prejudice exists 'out there' in its viewer.[1] That's its tension. No one gets to feel neutral about another person's body.

'The Benefits Supervisor Sleeping' is an exemplary visualisation of *désœuvrement*: the philosophical concept of worklessness discussed in the previous chapter. In its resistance to the idealising sublimation of the traditional nude, it gestures to an absence of *the work*, in the sense that it refuses the status of the work of art as great masterpiece or object of classical beauty. In its content meanwhile, it seems pulled between two political positions on the idea of worklessness in the sense of unemployment. On the one hand, a 'left' reading might see the benefits supervisor as an allegory for the hypocrisy of a system that demands we work, while being the very image of physical idleness itself. As Walter Benjamin observed, in Franz Kafka's fictions, government workers are always somehow lazy, grubby, and sloppily turned out, such 'that one could almost regard them as enormous parasites'.[2] And isn't there something of Kafka in the way the lumpy body and the lumpy sofa resemble each other? Gregor Samsa woke up as an 'enormous vermin'; Tilley wakes up as an enormous sofa. A right-wing viewer of the painting could be drawn to the benefit supervisor's maternal hand apparently offering her breast in her sleep, making her the bad, overbearing mother representing the nanny state (and, perhaps, at the same time, the benefits-dependent single mother, the *bête noire* of then-Prime Minister, John Major's 'Back to Basics' agenda). Simultaneously, in her near-foetal position she is another avatar of the moralisation of worklessness: the obese child, bloated out of proportion on junk food by her irresponsible parents.

Tilley worked for job centres around north and central London between 1978 and 2015. Her career began just prior to the transformation in the status of employment in political discourse in the West that characterised the neoliberal turn of the 1980s, and ended, as far as Britain is concerned, on the eve of the new Conservative majority government's shambolic rolling out of 'Universal Credit': an approach aimed at merging tax credit for the low waged with unemployment and incapacity benefits.[3] As for the painting, Tilley sat for Freud over the years just prior to New Labour's 1997 victory, and we suggest that the ambivalences we have identified in the paintings are shared in the political status of unemployment in that moment more generally.

As Nancy Fraser and Linda Gordon wrote at the time, these years marked the culmination of a long change in the notion of 'dependency'. In the seventeenth century, the *independence* of 'out-of-doors' (non-resident) servants made them an object of anxiety ('much as the anomalous "dependence" of "welfare mothers" does today'). In the industrial era, by contrast, 'those who aspired to full membership in society would have to distinguish themselves from the pauper, the native, the slave, and the housewife' – each now figured as avatars of a newly undesirable concept of *dependency* – 'in order to construct their independence', now the most desirable of conditions. While the paternalism of both high industrial and post-war welfare regimes could find ways of seeing the dependency of certain groups as proper and normative (the wife and children as 'dependants' within the family for instance), Fraser and Gordon argued the neoliberal 1980s and 1990s were eroding all positive cognates for the term, and indeed adding new negative ones. By a sleight of semantics, in the new discourse of *chemical, drug, and alcohol dependency*, dependency as an economic category became interchangeable with a pharmacological one.[4] We see this fudge completed today in the discourse of 'benefit dependency', an economic-cum-psychological category some have gone as far as to figure as a neurologically inscribed and heritable one, to be resolved only by controls on the reproductive rights of the unemployed.[5]

Yet despite the ideological contribution they and their outriders made to the representation of unemployment in the 1980s and early 1990s – and despite their policies' substantially increasing it – the right-wing governments of the period were actually conspicuous for their failure to substantially alter the structure of welfare.[6] The welfare queen was a favoured folk devil and justification for harsh cuts in the Reagan presidency, while Thatcherism was associated with a 'get on your bike and look for work' callousness towards the mass unemployment its policies created. But despite a devaluing of benefits and tightening of eligibility, the Thatcher years actually represented the peak of unconditional benefits paid by the state in Britain, including for the unemployed.[7] The first wave of neoliberalism's pursuit of the monetisation and marketisation of all spheres of life stumbled, then, at *désœuvrement*'s final hurdle: unemployment itself. Instead, in the US and parts of Europe, it fell to historical parties of the left to oversee this last push against welfare, as the jewel in the crown of their conversion to neoliberal orthodoxy: framed as the condition for their returning to power after long spells out of government. For Bill Clinton's New Democrats, the stated plan was to 'end welfare as we know it'; Tony Blair's New Labour – our focus in the next section – 'pushed the institutional "reform" of the welfare state to much deeper levels than even the Thatcher and Major governments'.[8] And in Germany, Gerhard Schröder's SPD pursued an equivalent programme of reforms, 'Agenda 2010' and 'Hartz IV', in the early 2000s.

## The end of unemployment

New Labour came to power proposing a set of 'New Deal' programmes – for lone parents, for those on disability benefits, for the young – combining compulsory training, work programmes, and some sanctions that were intended to be balanced by a new minimum wage and greater state funding for childcare. 'Jobseeker's Agreements' had been introduced at the end of the John Major government, initiating the recategorisation of unemployed people as 'jobseekers' that would define subsequent policy. From now on, payment of benefits would be highly conditional, and the state of being unemployed would be redesigned to be more like a job. While our account of the ideological basis for these changes is critical, it would be callous to underestimate how miserable being unemployed can be, and there were clearly those in New Labour who were perfectly well-intentioned about wishing to improve the chances of the marginalised. At the same time, it is hard to see how a party that had ruled out any rollback of the neoliberal restructuring of the economy since the late 1970s *could* have effectively intervened in the lives of people whose traditional job opportunities had disappeared. Lacking tools for more systemic intervention into the kind of work that was actually available, New Labour fell back on an inchoate, depoliticised, and sometimes euphemistic vocabulary clustered around the idea of 'jobseeking' that established conditions for damaging and illiberal effects that would only reach their full scale later on. As our critique runs, first, the party worked to a basically mystifying norm of 'community' and – in a repetition of the habit pointed out by Jean-Luc Nancy – made work identical with membership of it. Second, in characteristically neoliberal fashion, it tried to use welfare policy as a lever to create a new kind of subject capable of navigating conditions it claimed to be powerless to alter, even as it conspired to perpetuate those conditions.

A basic conflict and discrepancy between the two aspects of the 'Blair philosophy' – its 'communitarian side' and its 'modernising, targeting, moralising streak' – was observed early on by the cultural critic Stuart Hall. Hall remarked:

[I]t is difficult to believe fervently in 'the politics of community' and at the same time to hold unshakably to the view that the task of government is 'to help individuals to help themselves', especially when the ways of implementing each so often point in diametrically opposed directions.[9]

The entrance price for returning to the New Labour community was to consent to be transformed into the most aggressively anti-communitarian entrepreneurial subject. While community became New Labour's 'key leitmotif' and 'key collective abstraction', its binary opposite was 'social exclusion', a reformulation of long-term unemployment analogous to the redefinition of the unemployed as jobseekers.[10] In Ruth Levitas's analysis, the way in which the concept of social exclusion was adopted into New Labour's armoury and – after 2000 – into that of the European Union introduced a vagueness as to which intellectual tradition's use of the idea was being invoked by any given politician or group. In its academic origins, social exclusion had belonged to a broadly left 'redistributionist discourse', a broadly right 'moral underclass discourse', as well as a continental 'social integrationist discourse' focused on citizenship and work. Each tradition agreed that the social impact of poverty extended beyond simply having a low income, but had entirely different (and highly conflictual) ideas about what this impact consisted of, and how it could be remedied.[11]

This blurring of the term's political meaning had far-reaching ideological effects. The characteristic managerial jargon in the naming of New Labour's new 'Social Exclusion Unit' provided cover for the fact that it sometimes drew on the more dehumanising and victim-blaming frame of the 'moral underclass' tradition. A key voice of this trend was the American political scientist Charles Murray, whose view that certain kinds of poverty are genetic in origin (meaning that welfare programmes are bound to fail) and that – on average – lower IQ scores for black people are biologically inherent, did not prevent him being critically welcomed by elements in the New Labour milieu.[12] Certainly, his essentialising and biologising 'underclass' vocabulary dominated representations of the party's policies in the British media. A further problem was that the metaphor of social exclusion in general falsely implied a main 'included' body of society that was suffering no such problems, when in fact inequality among the 'in' group of the employed was considerable and growing, and the divide between many of the 'included' and the definitely 'excluded' was highly porous. As for 'community' – both the cure for the excluded and their projected destination – anyone who tried to be specific about what it entailed ended up resorting to what Richard Seymour describes as 'the values of a provincial fifties suburb'.[13] Concerned talk of a withdrawal from citizenship on the part of the long-term unemployed was also self-fulfilling, for it licensed the extra-legal and illiberal criminalisation of everyday life on estates and in town centres in the form of curfews and Antisocial Behaviour Orders, alienating and stigmatising the 'excluded' yet further. Fear that such people had slipped out of the citizenry justified treating them as less than citizens. As such, in what Richard Power Sayeed has represented as a consistent pattern in New Labour rhetoric, ideas with a partially radical and left-wing heritage were transformed into a cover for de-politicising or even actively reactionary tendencies.[14]

As Peter Mandelson summarised the approach, it was 'about more than poverty and unemployment. It [was] about being cut off from what the rest of us regard as normal life'.[15] But what counts as 'normal life' is not a static given. Rather, it is under continuous construction and reinforcement. The problem might be better understood with reference to Anthony Giddens, the celebrated sociologist who, as one of New Labour's 'few intellectual ornaments', did most to provide the appearance of intellectual substance to Blair's broadly opportunistic programme.[16] Giddens's pre-New Labour works already anticipated its distinctive *Weltanschauung*. 'In conditions of high modernity', Giddens wrote in 1991, 'we all not only follow lifestyles, but in an important sense are forced to do so – we have no choice but to choose ... [and] the more post-traditional the setting in which an individual moves, the more lifestyle concerns the very core of self-identity, its making and remaking'.[17] In contrast to the 'subcultures' posited by Birmingham School cultural studies in the 1960s and 1970s, there is little possibility that Giddens's 'lifestyles' might be actively altered by those who end up living them: they are simply imposed by a 'post-traditional' culture presented as unchangeable fact. Similarly, while hinting at the coercive violence of a system where 'we have no choice but to choose', Giddens does not make the qualification – as David Harvey does in his analysis of neoliberalism – that within such a system we 'are not supposed to choose to construct strong collective institutions (such as trade unions) ... [and] most certainly should not choose to associate to create political parties with the aim of forcing the state to intervene in or eliminate the market'.[18]

Applied to welfare, such a one-sided theory of the relationship between culture and subject could only conclude that an 'overbearing welfare state cannot equip individuals with the necessary capacity to navigate life successfully' and that welfare must be recalibrated 'to assist individuals to cope with new and changed risks'.[19] Sure enough, as Tom Slater describes, under New Labour 'workfarist policies were presented as "options" where "client groups" could "rationally choose" what they felt was best for them, even if to "stay at home on full benefit", to use the words of Gordon Brown, was not an option'.[20] If life in New Labour's 'high modernity' could indeed feel like a whirl of lifestyles, in which it was 'psychologically crucial' for subjects to adopt the 'protective cocoon' of continuous 'risk profiling' to be able to choose between, it said more about the party's obsession with imposing a simulacrum of consumer 'choice' in more and more spheres of life, than about any normative accuracy of Giddens's theory.[21]

In practice, qualifying the unemployed to navigate 'risk' involved 'cocooning' them in micro-management, as well as the transformation of non-work into a kind of para-work. Benefits officers like Sue Tilley were re-branded as 'personal advisers', 'whose job entail[ed] monitoring and liaising with claimants to speed their return to paid employment', alongside private firms paid to run training schemes.[22] The unemployed were literally 'put to work', in that the management of their activities became yet another hitherto unmonetised sphere of life newly opened out to private capital extraction. As Ivor Southwood describes, the experience of unemployment itself was 'turned into a pastiche of a job, complete with mock workplace, clocking in and out times, and managers to report to'.[23] This change could be seen as a formalisation of the 'work-for-labour' that to a greater or lesser extent always surrounds labour: the work performed by a worker in order to be in a position to sell her labour on the labour market in the first place. Only now, it was endowed with the formality of a boss, a workplace, and – in the implicit redefinition of benefits themselves – a wage.[24]

Slater outlines the 'substantial interdisciplinary empirical and theoretical literature' that has found that the American welfare reforms that provided the model for these changes in the UK 'do not lift people out of poverty, but rather remove them from welfare rolls, expand dramatically the contingent of the working and non-working poor, and affect their daily existence negatively in almost every way imaginable, aggravating extant class, racial and gender fractures in society'.[25] As we argue in this chapter's final section, such effects have come to be realised under subsequent governments to an extent that justifies a totally new vocabulary for talking about employment and unemployment.

## 'I would prefer not to'

In Patrick Kack-Brice's horror movie *Creep* (2014), an aspiring film director takes a job advertised online, which requires him to drive out to a woodland cottage to make a memorial film for a purportedly terminally ill employer to leave as a message to his unborn son. The 'found footage' is what the viewer sees. The employer's eccentric behaviour becomes more and more troubling as the job proceeds, and suffice to say, the film concludes with the employer – revealed as a serial killer – closing the door on a cupboard full of DVDs of victims who have effectively been tricked into creating the films of their own deaths. *Creep* thus reverses the logic of the founding texts of such meta-horror movies, Alfred Hitchcock's *Psycho* and Michael Powell's *Peeping Tom* (both 1960). Whereas the scandalous intimacy between the camera and the killer's gaze in those films had the effect of equating cinema and murder (rather literally in *Peeping Tom*: the murderer's blades are attached to a camera which is used to capture his victims' final moments), in *Creep* it is the hidden workers of film-making itself who are the quarry.

A kind of meta-cinema, then, *Creep* is in some ways less cinematic than a real-life American case it subtly recalls. In 2011, Richard Beasley, a down-on-his-luck preacher fleeing prostitution and drug charges, decided to find a new way to support himself in the informal online economy increasingly normalised since the financial crash.[26] Advertising on

Craigslist – a platform for anonymised adverts for goods and services – Beasley claimed to be seeking a permanent caretaker for a secluded Ohio farm, 'used mainly as a hunting preserve, overrun with game', with 'a stocked three-acre pond', 'some beef cattle', and the 'nearest neighbour a mile away'. Beasley met with candidate after candidate out of the hundred-plus who applied, screening for age, close family, and how connected to their communities they were. One at a time, the successful candidates were instructed to meet Beasley and a young accomplice, bringing with them a vehicle and any portable property of value. Beasley killed three men that way (another escaped), selling whatever they brought. The crime represented a strange nexus of forces coinciding at that moment. Both murderer and victim were in some way products of the post-2008 recession, or were at least moved to a certain recklessness by its conditions; and both were taking up the new digital 'platform' economy's invitation to find business in otherwise inaccessible relationships. Beasley might even have claimed to be acting like a perfect gig economy entrepreneur. His algorithm-like identification of a huge reserve army of unskilled, unemployed, middle-aged white men, unmarried or divorced, missed by no one, and desperate to believe in the impossible American pastoral he conjured, was also in some ways vindicated by later events.[27] This was exactly the constituency to which Donald Trump appealed, tipping the balance against the Democrats in Ohio and Rust Belt states like it.

A hipster in his thirties, *Creep*'s fictional victim seems far from Beasley's forgotten men, and the difference is compounded in *Creep 2*, where the protagonist is a young YouTuber who responds to the serial killer's unnerving invitation in the hope of getting some good content for her flailing channel. Yet the comparison of these three positions implied in *Creep*'s twist on the Beasley case sets up a pattern of precariousness and personal vulnerability that cuts across generational and class lines. Coding the movie as a fiction of the platform capitalism recession also gives it a surreptitious answer when the viewer makes the cries conventional to all horror movie audiences as the tension builds: 'why is he staying?!', 'you'd just leave wouldn't you?!', 'get out while you can!'. In the gig economy, it can be difficult to say 'I would prefer not to' to a job, however strange, risky, or impossible.

In November 2011 – days before Beasley's arrest in Akron, Ohio – Occupy Wall Street supporters in Manhattan's Zuccotti Park were performing a group reading of Herman Melville's *Bartleby, the Scrivener* (1853), the canonical American short story and totem text for the anti-work movement.[28] The story depicts an odd and withdrawn law clerk who bewilders the employer-narrator one day by refusing to perform any task he is commanded to do, repeatedly and simply replying: 'I would prefer not to'. This foundational refuser of work is discovered to be secretly living in the law offices he refuses to labour in (in Zuccotti Park they said he was 'occupying' them), which eventually leads to his arrest and death in prison. Finally, the narrator-employer hears that Bartleby had previously worked in a 'Dead Letter Office', responsible for destroying letters whose recipients, unbeknownst to the sender, were already dead when the letter arrived. Was Bartleby's subsequent career the result of the trauma of this most harrowingly alienated of labours? The text prefers not to commit, though Melville periodically implies that the bourgeois employer-narrator – for all his performance of profound awe at Bartleby's fate – is quite out of his depth when it comes to interpreting the events of his own story.

The narrative mileage *Bartleby* derives from its 'I would prefer not to' finds a precise reversal in *Creep*'s resigned compliance in the face of a job offer it would be unwise to accept. Yet we should pause before claiming for *Creep* the novelty of an updated *Bartleby* for the gig economy era. The fact is that Melville's own time already yields many examples of such fictional 'anti-Bartlebys'. Melville's tale of a surprising refusal of work can be read alongside this less celebrated, more surreptitious genre of stories, which take their energy precisely from characters *failing* or being unable to act like Bartleby and make such a refusal in the face of impossible, ridiculous, unappealing, or too-good-to-be-true kinds of work. We could include here Charles Dickens's *Martin Chuzzlewit*, where Tom Pinch, abandoned by his exploitative employer Pecksniff, journeys to London, only to find a job offer already waiting for him. The job is described by an intermediary:

'The salary was small, being only a hundred pounds a year, with neither board nor lodging, still the duties were not heavy, and there the post was. Vacant, and ready for your acceptance'.

'Good gracious me!', cried Tom; 'a hundred pounds a year!'

The job is too good to be true, and is the weirder for the employer's offer seeming to have come out of thin air:

'The strangest part of the story … is this. I don't know this man from Adam; neither does this man know Tom'.[29]

The gothic or sinister potential in Tom Pinch's situation is then exploited by the several *Sherlock Holmes* mysteries initiated by a similar exchange:

If these people had strange fads and expected obedience on the most extraordinary matters, they were at least ready to pay for their eccentricity. Very few governesses in England are getting a hundred a year. Besides, what use was my hair to me? Many people are improved by wearing it short and perhaps I should be among the number. ('The Copper Beeches')

It seemed altogether past belief that anyone … would pay such a sum for doing anything so simple as copying out the *Encyclopaedia Britannica*. ('The Red-Headed League')

'We have judged it best that you should come late. It is to recompense you for any inconvenience that we are paying you, a young and unknown man, a fee which would buy an option from very heads of your profession. Still, of course, if you would like to draw out of the business, there is plenty of time to do so'.

I thought of the fifty guineas, and of how very useful they would be to me.

'Not at all', said I, 'I shall be very happy to accommodate myself to your wishes'. ('The Engineers' Thumb')[30]

There is Jonathan Harker's increasingly awful experience in Transylvania at the start of Bram Stoker's *Dracula*, which nonetheless does not put him off his commission:

What sort of grim adventure was it on which I had embarked? Was this a customary incident in the life of a solicitor's clerk sent out to explain the purchase of a London estate to a foreigner?[31]

And a whole category of the 'don't take it' job is the situation of many governesses with odd employers in nineteenth-century fiction, concluding with Henry James's *The Turn of the Screw*:

'For several applicants the conditions had been prohibitive. They were, somehow, simply afraid. It

sounded dull – it sounded strange; and all the more
so because of his main condition'.

'Which was – ?'

'That she should never trouble him – but never,
never: neither appeal nor complain nor write about
anything; only meet all questions herself, receive
all moneys from his solicitor, take the whole thing
over and let him alone'.[32]

As we saw in Chapter 1, the industrial era is often associated with an increasing standardisation of employment
in the West; yet these examples suggest the period's fascination with the plentiful hinterland of exploitative,
unaccountable forms of short-term employment. The
platform capitalist gig economy, and the fictions that
come with it, have brought these nineteenth-century
beginnings to their conclusion. You can disappear from
work. Your work can make you disappear. And Bartleby
can't say no.

Occupy's joyful group reading was the latest in a long
line of activists and philosophers who have taken strength
from Bartleby's heroic passivity and wrongfooting of his
employer.[33] And yet as Southwood has noted, we should
today have more reservation about throwing ourselves in
with Bartleby's example.

If Bartleby had been an agency worker the fiction
would have turned out rather differently. If one

fancifully imagines a temporary data enterer who preferred not to perform the tasks assigned to him, this would present today's office manager with no such terrible insight.[34]

At a time of the complete disposability of the worker, the 'bullshit' nature of much of our work ('copying out the *Encyclopaedia Britannica*'), and the vulnerability – as Beasley's victims found – that this imposes on us, it may be that the 'other' tradition of anti-Bartlebys constitutes the one we should be turning to. Bartleby dies. But not without claiming the obsessed fascination of his employer, colonising the very speech of everybody around him (all the characters end up compulsively using the verb 'prefer'), and positioning himself as one of the great objects of interpretive labour in American literature.[35] It is not so, as our next section proposes, for the Bartlebys of today.

### *Malemployment* and *disemployment*

In an account of factory life in Bolton, Lancashire in the 1890s, the journalist C. Allen Clarke reflects:

> [E]re the speed of the machinery was accelerated to the present pitch, the spinners had time for a chat, and even a nap at their work; while the weavers could snatch a page of reading from a book, or do knitting or sewing, but not so today. In some places they

are even 'timed' when using the 'conveniences'; and only allowed so many minutes for nature's necessities, being fined if exceeding the limit fixed.

The yet-earlier forms of industrial labour Clarke looks mistily back to involve a comingling of work with our 'personal' selves. Today's critiques of post-industrial labour often focus (as we do in Chapter 3) on how it demands we make use in our work of aspects of our private identities, emotions, and bodies that previous labour models left to 'free time'. Yet in an inverted image of the all-colonising tendencies of such emotional labour today, Clarke imagines early industrial textiles as in some ways redeemed by the idea that it was not insistently separate from activities the workers would like to be doing anyway. Chatting, reading, knitting, and even napping are stitched into the working day, in an idealised balance of work and life that borders on the unalienated. Clarke contrasts this with the situation of his own late nineteenth century, which will be familiar to anyone in low-paid service work now. There is some grim scatological humour in the contrast Clarke sets up. The workers would be happy if they could bring their 'private' knitting and reading to work: industry responds by taking account of their shits in its profits. For Clarke, this pattern even extends to the workers' holidays, which no longer exist in opposition to work, but have become its quasi-medicalised concomitant: 'the factory young men ... freely confessed that they saved up money for holidays, for no other purpose but that of recruiting their health in order to keep up at their work during the rest of the year'.[36]

In twenty-first-century Britain, we are told that more people are in work than ever, and that those few stragglers who remain out of work are being returned to productive society by a streamlined acceleration of the 1990s welfare reforms called 'Universal Credit'. Earlier, we argued that the ideological mission of the 1990s welfare reforms was not merely to reduce the numbers of unemployed, but to eradicate the concept altogether by extending work into the condition of worklessness itself: reconceiving unemployment as just another category to be 'put to work' in the lifework regime. Here we claim that the material result of this is that a simple opposition between employment and unemployment – with their respective moralised cognates of success and failure, health and sickness, autonomy and dependency, prosperity and struggle – can no longer be sustained. Great numbers of people living lives that would formerly have been categorised as belonging to either state might now be better understood as existing in *malemployment* or *disemployment*.

To be *malemployed* is to perform work that is insufficiently remunerated to live on, anti-social, precarious, physically and mentally unhealthy, contains substantial unpaid elements, is invasive, micromanaged and undignified, and/or sustains 'in-work poverty': work that is, which super-charges the deleterious practices seen by Clarke in his account of factory work at the end of the nineteenth century. Our second category, *disemployment*, meanwhile, is the experience of those who have been removed from unemployment figures, are not collecting benefits, but who have not reappeared within the job market; those in other words, who have simply been expelled or cancelled from the official economy as such.

A decade after the financial crash of 2008, Philip Alston, the United Nations Special Rapporteur on extreme poverty and human rights, produced a report on the condition of Britain's poor. It found a fifth of the population currently living in poverty and predicted that half of all children will be living in poverty by 2022 failing serious change.[37] The report followed the underexposed but historically extraordinary move by Britain's Office for National Statistics (ONS), which, based on the period 2014–2016, revised its predictions for life expectancy in Britain downward for the first time in more than a century. Between 2015 and 2017, around 70,000 people died that the ONS's models had previously assumed would live. The first wave of deaths were older women, with older men and then all people of working age increasingly dominating the statistics year on year.[38] How can we explain such destruction, when the Conservative Party's 2017 manifesto claims both that 'employment is at a record high' and that 'work is the best route out of poverty'?

Britain, in common with much of Europe, had indeed recovered its pre-crash employment levels by 2015, and unemployment continued to fall in subsequent years. Yet as Jason Heyes and others have noted, while 'the UK government is fixated with the quantity of jobs in the economy and the rates of employment and unemployment in aggregate', these conventional metrics 'reveal nothing about the quality of jobs and whether they provide workers with a means of achieving an acceptable standard of living'. 'Skills' remains the keyword in policy conversations about how people can improve their work and get ahead, yet 'many workers find that the skills and knowledge that they possess are not fully utilized in their jobs'.[39] A great number of us are over-skilled for the de-skilled work that is actually available, and no amount of individualised retraining will magic into existence secure high-quality jobs for everyone who is qualified for them. Such 'underemployment', where an officially employed worker cannot get as many hours as she wants or needs, or is performing work well below the skills and training the state has encouraged her to acquire, is occurring alongside a partner phenomenon of 'overemployment', where workers must take more jobs or more hours than is bearable in order to sustain a minimal level of living. A similar dynamic is found in differences between earning groups. As David Frayne observes, 'we are confronted with ... a perverse situation in which the highest-ranking workers are plagued by long hours, whilst growing numbers of people suffer because their labour power is no longer useful'.[40]

Under/overemployment are terms gaining traction in academic analyses of work, and tend to be framed – as in

Heyes's study just quoted – as a problem of 'well-being', from the perspective of asking what the 'just right' amount of work, remuneration, and level of skill would be to keep workers happy. We suggest that a tougher approach is needed, one that identifies official indifference – or worse – to the question of whether one should be earning enough to support oneself in order to count as employed, as symptomatic of a wider phenomenon of *malemployment*. The concept collects what are ordinarily seen as quite separate negative phenomena. We argue that a collective term is needed to recognise these as the collective outcome of a situation where work is defined only as value extraction, or as a quasi-moral end in itself, and so leaves all questions about its purpose in our common lives to one side. *Malemployment* might be work falsely categorised as self-employment, so that it has all the demands of employee life, with none of the security. It might be micromanaged, as in coffee chains where workers' emotional behaviour is constantly monitored, with collective punishment for teams with glum members; or as it is for call centre workers, who, like their industrial forebears in Clarke's account, find their bathroom breaks put on a clock. It might be work where a layer of team leaders or supervisors – impotent and under-payed themselves – are incentivised to use the withholding of shifts and other underhand tactics to discipline colleagues.[41] It might – for all the talk of the unhealthiness of unemployment – be chronically bad for our health in itself. In the UK 1.2 million people reported suffering from work-related illnesses in 2013/14, so that, as for Clarke's factory workers, all free time (and much company money for 'well-being' programmes) is spent ameliorating its bad effects.[42] And it might be at the heart of a perverse mini ecosystem of *malemployment* of its own, such as it is for those forced, as a condition of their benefits to work at foodbanks, so that they end up 'both a foodbank user and a volunteer, ... preparing food parcels for themselves'.[43]

*Malemployment*, then, brings together practices that cut across conventional class and social boundaries. But perhaps more remarkably, it also encompasses kinds of work status from both sides of the traditional employment/unemployment divide. *Malemployment* breaks with the conventional binary oppositions relating to employment/unemployment and creates cases where it is hard to firmly tell the difference. In *malemployment*, employed and unemployed alike can be made insecure, poor and unhealthy by their work and lack of it. At the bottom end, employed and unemployed can even perform exactly the same work in the same branches of the same companies, eat from the same foodbanks, and return at night to the same sheltered accommodation. For all that the political agents that have fomented these developments represent themselves as working against inefficient state intervention, both kinds of *malemployment* have to be subsidised by the state: directly in the benefits supplied to unpaid and unemployed workfare participants, indirectly in tax credits and other in-work benefits for the poverty-pay worker (not to mention the cost to the NHS in work-related illness).

Like New Labour in 1997, the Conservative–Liberal Democrat Coalition came to government in 2010 with a raft of new welfare measures. New Labour made inroads into the commodification of unemployment and its reconceptualisation as a kind of work in itself, but the Coalition was considerably more ambitious. Iain Duncan Smith was appointed Secretary of State for Work and Pensions following six years on the backbenches as chairman of the Social Justice Policy Group, which advanced conservative solutions to poverty. Before that, Duncan Smith had endured a short and unpopular tenure as Conservative Party leader in opposition, conspicuous for its aspiration to 'resume' the Thatcherite project 'where it left off', and – in the words of one of his shadow ministers redolent of the radical right – 'end the serfdom of the NHS monopoly' with a US-style private insurance system.[44] In government, Duncan Smith oversaw new workfare schemes that attempted to make unemployment yet more indistinguishable from work. As these measures set in over the course of 2012, one began to see adverts for supermarket shift work with pay listed as 'JSA [Jobseeker's Allowance] + expenses', workers on short-term contracts were dropped in favour of workfare participants, and recruitment freezes were imposed by companies participating in workfare schemes.[45] Public outcry and concerted activism tempered sanctions for those refusing to participate in these schemes and pushed supermarkets to formally hire more of those who did. But the point is that this was a welfare regime that inaugurated itself with a programme that was at best indifferent to the obvious objection: *either there is work to be done or there isn't*. And if there is, it ought to be properly paid. So much for unemployment's resemblance to employment: to take the inverse – employment that resembles unemployment – as of 2018, 55 per cent (in London, 60 per cent) of those declared homeless and living in temporary accommodation are working.[46] To be employed is no longer any guarantee against the historical living conditions of the most abject unemployment.

There is justification, then, for revising the category of unemployment as now belonging in a spectrum with employment – no longer as qualitatively separate from it – and forms of both as constituting the category of *malemployment*. What, though, of *disemployment*? One of the ironies of the direction of travel on welfare established by New Labour is that its focus on the inadequate 'citizenship' of the socially excluded (and ambition to restore it to them) has now been inverted, so that a kind of revocation of citizenship has become one of the welfare system's explicit disciplinary powers. The people on whom this discipline is effected we propose to call the 'disemployed'. Since the introduction of the National Insurance Act in 1911, the unemployed could, under special circumstances, be indirectly fined through the withholding of benefits. As of 2012, however, Duncan Smith placed sanctions at the heart of the benefits system, radically increasing the period benefits could be withheld for and the range of sanctionable offences, as well as extending sanctions from the unemployed to single parents, long-term sick, and disabled people. 'While sanctions used to be applied to unemployed people who were held to be responsible for losing their jobs', observes Michael Adler, 'they are now much more concerned with the job-seeking behaviour of all claimants who are not in employment and with conformity to the administrative requirements that are imposed by personal advisers'.[47] The system for adjudicating who is excluded from benefits in this way is not effective. Sanctionable offences – like assessments of the fitness of individual sick and disabled people for work – are decided by outsourced companies who are necessarily motivated by profit rather than fairness towards those in the system. In 2018 it was reported that nearly 70 per cent of claimants who appealed decisions barring them from disability benefits were successful in their claim that they had been denied wrongly. Forty per cent of those initially refused do not appeal because it would be too stressful.[48]

Universal Credit, the baroque system conceived to bring Duncan Smith's initial reforms to completion, has expanded the ranks of the *disemployed* yet further. Southwood argues that the system 'is *designed* to be impractical and convoluted and to put low-paid and unemployed claimants at risk of debt and homelessness through routine payment delays and arbitrary sanctions'.[49] Alston's comments in the UN report on the 'digital by default' requirements of the system seem to agree, as Alston 'wonders why some of the most vulnerable and those with poor digital literacy had to go first in what amounts to a nation-wide digital experiment'; adding that 'we are witnessing the gradual disappearance of the post-war British welfare state behind a webpage and an algorithm'.[50] Imagine for a moment that we accept the imperative to bring down the welfare bill and to encourage those who can to work; and also that we concede that the system is entirely well-intentioned and efficient. It remains impossible to reconcile the routine use of benefits sanctions – generally meaning the withdrawal of an individual's sole income – with a belief in the liberal state's responsibility to guarantee a baseline living standard for its citizens. Benefits cannot at once be the guaranteed baseline living standard *and* a legitimate lever of discipline to be withdrawn. Given how profound its implications are for the very basis of liberalism, Del Roy Fletcher and Sharon Wright note that there has been 'surprisingly little political debate' on this question.[51] And yet the outcome is the production of a *disemployed* caste, who – like the many case studies in Jeremy Seabrook's book, *Cut Out: Living without Welfare* (2016) – are still not in work, may be quite unable to work, but who have now been excluded from the benefits system. People, that is, who have been removed from the gaze of the ordinary economy altogether.[52]

So far from returning the disadvantaged to the condition Mandelson described as 'what the rest of us regard as normal life', the post-2012 reforms have extended the quasi-criminalisation of ordinary activities (claimants who make simple mistakes in complex bureaucratic processes are punished automatically, or have debts imposed in reprisal for overpayments made in error by the Department for Work and Pensions itself) and created a substantially new mechanism by which swathes of the population can be ejected from the legitimate economy and 'normal life' altogether. To draw on the work of Saskia Sassen, it is possible to frame this invention of *disemployment* as part of a wider crisis of the liberal order based around new kinds of 'expulsions':

> There is a de facto redefinition of 'the economy' when sharp contractions are gradually lost to standard measures. The unemployed who lose everything – jobs, homes, medical insurance – easily fall off the edge of what is defined as 'the economy' and counted as such. So do small shop and factory owners who lose everything and commit suicide ... These trends redefine the space of the economy. They make it smaller and expel a good share of the unemployed and the poor from standard measures. Such a redefinition makes 'the economy' presentable, so to speak, allowing it to show a slight growth in its measure of GDP per capita. The reality at ground level is more akin to a kind of economic version of ethnic cleansing in which elements considered troublesome are dealt with by simply eliminating them.[53]

Sassen's work associates such expulsions of individuals performed inside economies with those performed without – wars that obliterate countries' whole infrastructure, aggressive immigration controls and a growing relaxedness about making people stateless or separating children from parents – and the expulsions involved in land being made unliveable by climate change and more direct forms of pollution.[54] Through this frame of new international manifestations of 'expulsion', the creation of the *malemployed* and *disemployed* in Britain could be seen as parts of the population of the developed world being pressed to join the 60 per cent of the world population that already sustain themselves outside the protections of the formal economy (most of them in the developing world).[55] At home, the *disemployed* find an analogue in the tolerance for expulsions behind the Grenfell Tower disaster and the Windrush deportation scandal, widely attributed to the government's policies of delegating public spending cuts to local government, and the 'Hostile Environment' immigration policy (discussed in Chapter 1) respectively. The violence resulting from the redefinition of unemployment since the 1990s is precisely the violence Nancy identified as emerging when labour and community are treated as identical.

# 3

# We Young-Girls

At a conference in San Diego in 2014, the new media artist Laurel Ptak staged an exhibition for a semi-fictional
political campaign, 'Wages for Facebook'. The associated
website manifesto, a text set in automatically scrolling,
capitalised letters, claims that in the paradigmatic form
of Facebook, capitalism has 'CONVINCE[D] US THAT
IT IS A NATURAL, UNAVOIDABLE AND EVEN
FULFILLING ACTIVITY TO MAKE US ACCEPT
UNWAGED WORK'. We do not normally think of our
free time use of social media and other digital platforms as
work, even though we are increasingly aware of the kinds
of value extraction platform owners derive from it: in the
unwitting training we provide for algorithms by every
click, in the attention we garner by our social media posts,
and more universally, the potential surplus value of our
data. 'WE MUST ADMIT THAT CAPITAL HAS BEEN

VERY SUCCESSFUL IN HIDING OUR WORK', the manifesto reads.[1] Where the previous chapter showed how even unemployment has been 'put to work', Ptak's artwork suggests that developments in platform capitalism turn even our most idle online surfing, gaming, and posting into a kind of alienated labour.

'Wages for Facebook' can be read next to the work of scholars who place our unpaid interactions on digital platforms under the discrete umbrella term 'digital labour'. 'Internet usage is productive consumption or prosumption in the sense that it creates value and a commodity that is sold', explains the term's coiner Christian Fuchs.[2] Others are more cautious about extending the concept of wage labour to whatever we do online. While in both cases, a capitalist owner derives surplus value from the activity of others, the experience of making cars is not exactly like taking pictures of our pets, and attending an office team meeting is not like group chatting with our friends. For Nick Srnicek, it is important 'to draw distinctions between interactions done on platforms and interactions done elsewhere', lest we topple into a nominalism where 'work becomes inseparable from non-work' and '*all* social interaction becomes free labour for capitalism'.[3]

Ptak's work, in its central conceit, points beyond the impasse: 'Wages for Facebook' is a near word-for-word transcription of passages from Silvia Federici's manifesto, *Wages Against Housework* (1975) that replaces the word 'housework' in the original with 'Facebook'.[4] As

Ptak's gesture disarmingly suggests, dilemmas of how to interpret work in its domestic and digital iterations are in fact sufficiently identical not to require a revision of wording. Likewise, the strategies for analysing and resisting the former might inform the ones aimed at the latter.[5] Federici's manifesto was a contribution to the International Feminist Movement's 1970s campaign for wages for housework. The contention was that housework and reproductive labour, despite being as structurally necessary to capitalist profits as waged labour, had been successfully dressed up as a woman's god-given task and no kind of work at all. In her manifesto, Federici harbours no illusion that putting a price on household tasks would in itself liberate housewives. The aim is political, and taken on as such by Ptak: 'THE WAGE AT LEAST RECOGNIZES THAT YOU ARE A WORKER. YOU CAN BARGAIN AND STRUGGLE AROUND AND AGAINST THE TERMS AND THE QUANTITY OF THAT WAGE, THE TERMS AND THE QUANTITY OF THAT WORK'.

In the first instance, the 'wages for housework' campaign is a reminder of the fact that capitalism is a form of economic exploitation never confined to the wage relation. Since capitalism depends on perpetual growth, it must maximise exploitation; inevitably it seeks to find profit in human activities outside the one acknowledged by the wage, whatever form they may take. Unpaid domestic work, unequivocally arduous, produces surplus value for capitalists indirectly (in housing, feeding, and supporting waged workers and replenishing the workforce). Unpaid digital labour, inversely, usually experienced as leisure or convenience, directly produces surplus value for capitalists in the form of monetisable data. 'Labour' fits neither activity perfectly; and while they are both exploitative, they are not exploitative in the same way. Nobody is suggesting that doing the laundry and social media updates are the same thing. What they have in common is that they are profitable activities normally invisible as such: imagining them as waged labour, whether as part of a concrete political programme or as a tactical gesture, renders them visible as a first step towards organising them differently.

So there are good political and economic reasons for taking seriously the idea of unwaged work online and elsewhere. But there is another aspect of Federici's argument without which the parallel between social media and housework must remain superficial. As she points out in *Wages Against Housework*, 'capitalism makes money out of our cooking, smiling, fucking' without causing rebellion, because in the home it is impossible to see 'where our work begins and ends, where our work ends and our desire begins'.[6] If, as Louise Toupin notes in her history of the International Feminist Movement, the idea behind the wage for housework was 'to establish a separation between the person and the work she was doing', this is a separation as difficult to access in the digital economy as it ever was, and remains, in housework.[7]

What is at stake here, beyond delivering free data, is not only that it is difficult to know whether what, at a given moment, you do online is friendship or labour, but rather that the 'self' produced in the process increasingly resembles a kind of surplus value, or rather, a kind of 'living currency', to use Pierre Klossowski's term. By farming our desires, capitalism not only gets free housework and free data, it also produces subjects who relate to themselves as commodities, online and offline.

One way to expand this idea has been the concept of the 'Young-Girl', advanced by the French anarchist collective, Tiqqun, in *Preliminary Materials for a Theory of the Young Girl* (2012). Originally published in 1999, *Preliminary Materials* proposed that a paradigmatic figure of the 'Young-Girl' had become the 'model citizen as redefined by consumer society since World War I'.[8] In the eighteenth and nineteenth centuries, young upper-class Western women took a peculiar position in society, since, rather than performing recognisable labour or overseeing that of others, their function was to labour specifically on *themselves*:

> You read, or have lessons, or otherwise improve your mind, till the middle of the day; take a walk before lunch, go for a drive with your aunt after, and have some kind of engagement in the evening.[9]

> No one can be really esteemed accomplished who does not greatly surpass what is usually met with.

A woman must have a thorough knowledge of
music, singing, drawing, dancing, and the modern languages, to deserve the word; and besides all
this, she must possess a certain something in her air
and manner of walking, the tone of her voice, her
address and expressions, or the word will be but
half-deserved.[10]

This was the work of a certain self-production, the cul-
tivation of appearance, social connections, manners, and
'attainments': kinds of ability – in needlework or drawing room recital for instance – that were practised and
cultivated primarily for the performance of feminine
accomplishment. Their only permissible pleasures were a
rigorously structured system of dances, games, and appear-
ances. This social position had its greatest articulation in
the novels of Jane Austen, which – at the start of the nineteenth century – managed to create a whole narrative form
out of the dilemmas of intelligent and enterprising women,
for whom society afforded no imperative other than that
they *be themselves*, and work hard at it.

Far from being simply superseded with the decline of
the gentry who principally practised it, for Tiqqun, the figure of the Young-Girl has instead been allowed to become
paradigmatic in the obligation we have all been placed
under to '*permanently self-valorize*': that is to say, to unite –
as Austen's young women did – our very selves with the
commodity form, and to make this the underpinning task

of all our labour.[11] For Tiqqun, at this point we are all Young-Girls, pushed into cultivating, remodelling, and valorising our image.

## Histories of the Young-Girl

'The Young-Girl is obviously not a gendered concept', Tiqqun state, 'all the old figures of patriarchal authority, from statesmen to bosses and cops, have become Young-Girlified, every last one of them, even the Pope'. The claim has only become more compelling since Tiqqun made it in 1999, before the rise of social media. They hadn't seen the pope's Instagram account, or the series *The Young Pope* (2016).[12] At the same time, taking the signifier 'young girl' and turning it into the emblem of the times evidently comes with theoretical risks that cannot be un-gendered.[13] Critics have, with justification, taken up *Preliminary Materials* for its misogyny. Heather Warren-Crow, for instance, frames Tiqqun's analysis as an example of a 'girl-phobic' habit, disappointingly persistent in radical cultural criticism, of associating all that the critic disapproves of with adolescence and femininity. Nina Power, meanwhile, is doubtful about the lack of agency and conscious discontent Tiqqun find in the Young-Girl, asking 'what, ultimately, would it mean to let the Young-Girl speak for herself and not through the categories imposed upon her by a culture that heralds her as the metaphysical apex of civilization while simultaneously denigrating her'?[14] While

Tiqqun are dismayed at the work of Young-Girlification undertaken by everybody under late capitalism, their feminist critics are dismayed that young women should seem to be blamed for this oppression – not only their own, but everybody else's – in Tiqqun's analysis.

It is of course possible to discuss capital's attempts at increasingly total fusion of personhood and market-value without leaning on young women to provide the requisite paradigm. If even the pope is a Young-Girl now, then why still mention girls at all? It strikes us as justified for at least two reasons. The first one lies in the continuing cultural centrality of the figure of the elevated-yet-denigrated 'girl' acknowledged by Power. In 2015, Jacqueline Rose pointed out the rise of an enormously popular type of fiction that specifically invites women, under the fig leaf of moments of revenge, to derive pleasure from protracted scenes of psychological and sexual violence against women. The diminutive 'girl' usually found in the titles of these works, she notes, is complicit in a gesture of diminishment that figures women as 'pliable' on the one hand and implicitly bad or stupid on the other, and so invites their sadistic punishment.[15] We might also recall here that for Sianne Ngai, signalling 'pliability' is a central feature of 'cuteness' as a dominant aesthetic category in contemporary commodity culture, and as such even posits it as the essential gesture of objectification: 'the more objectified the object, or the more visibly shaped by the affective demands and/or projections of the subject, the cuter'.[16] The squishable bath toy and girlified character both: exciting the 'desire to protect and cuddle' as well as aggression. It would seem that in a culture where everyone is under pressure to Young-Girlify, that is, to mould every aspect of their lives into optimum marketability, there is no shortage of Young-Girl cultural objects, and they are aimed at everyone, including women, in what appears to be an offer of compensatory sadism. Add to this often sadistic fetishising of the girl in our fictions and products, the vortex of online hostility generally directed at representative 'young girls', from outcries about discrimination against white masculinity to the denigration of a whole generation and their political concerns as those of 'triggered', anxious 'snowflakes', and it is clear that young women subject to misogynist violence will not be served by ignoring the cultural pull of the tropes mobilised in their names.

Meanwhile, Power's call to 'let the Young-Girl speak for herself' has apparently been answered, and to a hitherto unthinkable extent. In the #Metoo movement following sexual assault allegations against film producer Harvey Weinstein in October 2017, victims of the sexual violence of powerful men came forward on social media in their thousands. Welcome as the ensuing debate around sexual exploitation in and around work places has been, its limitations soon became apparent. Commentators have noted that in terms of material change, the group solidarity promised by the movement's slogan generally shrinks into individualised action, where perpetrators in high-profile cases are persecuted with little change in the systemic professional risks and the means of redress available to the most vulnerable.[17]

This failed promise of solidarity is mirrored in the performative requirements of the movement: 'Me, too' promises the relief of recognition without the burden of explanation – that you will be able to join the ranks of a group that fights for a common cause finally recognised as such. But access to the movement's benefits – the public pressure it can leverage on institutions and individual perpetrators – comes at the price not only of public exposure, but also of submission to the rules of genre not unlike those of the pseudo-feminist 'Young-Girl' potboilers critiqued by Rose two years earlier: you, too, will have to deliver lurid sexual detail, a tidy narrative arc, and situational detail calculated to convey to others the enjoyable, addictive rage that we might call, with Paul B. Preciado, 'pharmacopornographic': a marketable, irrefusable titillation effect that becomes its own end and defuses what may have been, and may still become, the effect of a common political cause. The angry Young-Girl is no longer the dismissed hysteric, the 'madwoman in the attic' of nineteenth-century fiction, and instead becomes the counterpart of the fetishised victim, a thrilling individualised spectacle, whether on social media, or in hyper-violent revenge fiction. The cultural mechanics of #Metoo thus reproduce crucial parts of the Young-Girl function: putting to work your sexuality alongside any other saleable part of your experience, *including* your revolt against sexual exploitation, and without the rewards of systemic change.

In a sense, the 'Young-Girl' always 'speaks for herself', because 'she' only exists as a number of social, economic, and cultural protocols that dictate the work we must undertake to surface into visibility under digital capitalism. While, in the impatience for material change, Power's attempt to strip away cultural and theoretical clutter to get to the *true* young girl, who is simply persecuted by 'a bunch of rich white men' is understandable, it runs the risk of the biological essentialism that fetishises young cis women on the one hand and the social homogenisation of their position, at the expense of class and global context, on the other. Instead, we might put the idea of Young-Girlification to use as a description of a hegemonic form of biopolitical submission required as the entry ticket to late capitalist culture; young cis women continue to be exploited as prominent avatars of it, but they do not describe its essence, nor, for that matter, the full range of people subject to sexual violence in the capitalist workplace. The 'Young-Girl', then, rather than blaming women, separates them from the cultural protocol associated with them, and yet offers some explanation for some forms of cultural and economic violence directed against them.

The second reason to stay with the Young-Girl as a critical tool is historical. It is impossible to ignore that Tiqqun themselves fall into the trap of reification when they make their supposedly emblematic abstraction the humanoid target of bog-standard misogyny.[18] What remains of interest in their theoretical wager, however, is directed the other way, towards the history of a cultural trap – and one that regards labour. In a rough and very brief introductory sketch, Tiqqun propose that the Young-Girl represents two elements, *youthitude* and *femininitude*, as regulatory ideals that allowed capitalism to integrate women and children, groups that were marginal to production in the twentieth-century West, as model consumers. When we try to assess the vagaries of today's lifework, it is worth looking to this social history of capital.

Others before Tiqqun have remarked on the special place of childhood and youth in the social conditions as well as the ideology of industrial capitalism. Social historians have documented how protective legislation against child labour in early twentieth-century Fordist America coincided with a new imperative in advertising to promote the idea of the child consumer. Max Horkheimer, writing in 1941, went as far as to argue, in psychoanalytic terms, that mass culture had undermined subject formation to the extent that the representative father figure on whom the young peg their battle with the society they enter had been 'replaced by the world of things' that addresses the child early and insidiously, with no room left to argue.[19] Meanwhile, unskilled young adults came into demand on the production line, displacing older workers whose specialised craft had become expensive and obsolete; not surprisingly, this proved a cultural moment where anxious age became the target for an expanding market of products connoting youth.[20] Writing in 1930, Siegfried Kracauer suspected that the youth fetish he identified in German popular culture was not only a reflection of a new prejudice against older workers in company policy, but a denial of death of a whole culture at a time where the lack of cultural and economic perspective makes youth the only bearable time of life.[21] Looking back to his early years in imperial Austria at the end of the nineteenth century, Stefan Zweig describes a bourgeois world where young men, for the sake of promotion, affected a slow walk, wore spectacles, grew beards, and tried to grow at least a little fat in order to attain the signifiers of dignified age.[22] The inversion of this scene, as the old become newly disposable in the rationalised workplace, is already nervously acknowledged in Thomas Mann's novella *Death in Venice* (1912). Among a group of holidaying trainee business clerks, the protagonist recognises with horror an old man, with dyed hair, make-up and fake teeth, dressed in the dandyish fashion and behaving in the ostentatiously blustering manner of his young colleagues.[23] Well before the 1950s and the association of youth with simultaneously rebellious and profitable counter-cultures, writers were identifying at least a triple place for the young under industrial capitalism; as malleable consumers, disposable workers, and as the purchasable promise of youthful hope.

Women have played an even more obviously paradigmatic part in the history of capitalist production's significant outsiders. The well-worn but important narrative of the invention of the housewife, also the basis of Federici's work discussed above, is instructive here: as manufacturing, from the eighteenth century onwards, increasingly took people out of the 'life, care, and home collective' of the smallholders, it also took out their traditional crafts, now learnt by machines. Those who remained at home, bereft of their productive tasks, were left on their own with the tasks of social reproduction – making babies, care and house work. As Angela Davis crucially points out, women were the losers of this split of home and production in a double sense; the work that they continued to do as housewives lost its social status, since, unlike the activities the factories had taken out of the home economy, it did not directly generate profit. Meanwhile the women who yet had to work for a wage were treated worse and paid less than men, since their presence in the public economy represented a transgression of their idealised, naturalised role in the home.[24] As capitalism and patriarchy united to render 'women's work' wageless and essentially workless, because natural, it made their place in- and outside the home more economically vulnerable and precarious than it had generally been in the home economy. Unsurprisingly, this left them perfect targets for the advertisement industry that, beginning in the 1920s, aggressively coached them to commodify their sexuality to maintain their access to the wages of men.[25]

What emerges from this history is a strange and haunting connection between desirability and disposability. Where Tiqqun point to the young and women as two separate groups that first, were marginal to production, and second, became model consumers (as well as models for advertising's principal fantasies), they sketch one convincing genealogy for Young-Girl self-commodifiers in the twenty-first century. What Tiqqun leave out is the glaring fact that when everybody turns Young-Girl under digital capitalism, at home as well as at work, they inherit their predecessors' precarious relation to capital alongside their strategies for survival. This, surely, is the crux of the history of capitalist production's outsiders – that increasing self-commodification comes alongside increasing precarity. As a tendency in employment structures, it has long been noted: Italian autonomists like Maurizio Lazzarato have pointed to the increasing predominance of 'immaterial labour', as forms of work that are either unaccounted for in the wage relation or generate no visible products, and are thus more easily exploited than traditional factory work. Both the ever-expanding service sector and the 'cognitive' labour of the digital economy, like data entry, are commonly cited examples for 'immaterial' work that is increasingly out-sourced, on-demand, and overall 'hyperexploitable'.[26] A significant related category in the discussion of 'immaterial' work has been 'affective labour', as any form of work that requires 'the creation and manipulation of affect' in others. It is usually undertaken at the cost of what Arlie Russell Hochschild has described, in the now canonical case of airline hostesses, as the 'emotional work' of managing and repressing the workers' own feelings, or, and often at the same time, as for Federici's housewife, at the cost of the messy engagement of her most private desires.[27] Finally, the idea of the 'feminization of labour' combines the predominance of service work, affective labour and increasing precarity: even referred to by some 1980s feminists as the 'housewifization' of work, it acknowledges the history discussed above.[28] What was once the work of those who were either placed outside the wage relation or hyper-exploited at its socio-cultural margins, has become the hegemonic model for today's digital economy.

There are 'Young-Girl' histories that take the link between socioeconomic margin and economic model even further. Preciado follows this logic in *Testo Junkie*, when he suggests that the paradigmatic workers of our time are the sex worker and the porn actor, representative of our economy in a general 'pornification of work': representative because in the first instance, 'work in the Post-Fordist society is always and in every case the sale of the force of communication and excitation produced by a living body – the sale of that body's *potentia gaudendi*'. Accordingly, the purpose of our work today is not to participate – as Tiqqun prefer to frame it – in the Debordian spectacle so much as it is to cause excitation, to addictively stimulate the production of endorphin, adrenaline, and other neurotransmitters in the bodies of others. This has always been true of sex, service, and entertainment industries, although the algorithmic narrowing, for example, in mainstream film production, chain restaurants, and keyword porn makes it more apparent. But it is also increasingly true of affective self-commodification in hierarchical relationships in the neoliberal workplace as well as on social media.

As Preciado puts it, 'in a porn-economy, there is no work that isn't destined to cause a hard-on'; everything we do 'must produce the effect of a fix'. He also stresses the radical precarity of sex workers; that, as in cases of trafficking and illegal migration, they often work from extreme positions of marginality, 'a majority of migrant bodies declared illegal and distinguished by lines of racialization and social exclusion', dehumanised to the point of the denial of citizenship. Preciado doesn't pursue the implication in detail, but there is a bleak warning in his description of how excluded people become 'penetrable bodies'. If the migrant sex workers of globalisation are the quintessential workers of our present and potential future economy, they are disposable to the point of legal non-existence and yet plugged into a global network for the distribution of images, or moved along global channels for the distribution of human bodies – absolute availability alongside absolute absence of right to citizenship. We have seen in Chapter 2 how this erosion of citizenship is an integral part of *disemployment*, the exclusion of large groups of the unemployed from official statistics and state assistance, and how this relates to Saskia Sassen's idea of global 'expulsions' of people from the economy, the polity and, in the case of climate catastrophes, from bare survival. Here, Preciado offers the chilling outlook that work itself, in what we might consider *malemployment*'s final conclusion, makes the worker at work not only precarious, but unaccounted for as an officially existing human being. The globalised sale of excitation renders human workers mechanical parts more than they ever were under unionised Fordism: 'there is no longer any competition between machine and worker. On the contrary: the worker is becoming a sexual biomachine'.[29] The link between an Instagram lifestyle entrepreneur selling make-up and illegal sex workers plugged into globalised technocapitalism, then, would not be simply that of self-commodifying sexuality, rejected out of bourgeois prudishness dressed up as socialism – it is rather that Young-Girlification, among other things, reduces work to the sort of addictive entertainment that is based on simple calculations for physical 'excitation/frustration' – so simple that its actors are totally fungible executors of a stimulation protocol.

Histories of the Young-Girl, then, can be understood as capitalism's successful implementation, from the eighteenth century to the present day, of an expansive regime of desirability as disposability, from the deskilled housewife to the migrant sex worker. Exploitation is not new, and for those able and willing to see it, the transatlantic slave trade, as the engine of capitalist expansion, has indicated the baseline of capitalist exploitation of work from the start. What has changed over the centuries is the extent to which the demand to perform individual desirability, via technologies of global distribution and communication, has spread from the economic margin to the centre even as it entrenches socioeconomic difference: Young-Girlification can account for the similarities between CEOs and webcammers in their performance of a certain kind of total availability within the same protocols of self-commodification, yet it also shows that this very similarity and cultural levelling is predicated on a social division so brutal it comes down to a human/non-human distinction. Yet, at the opposite extreme, the spread of colonisation of life by work, or what Michael Hardt calls the break-down of 'the division between culture and economy' has also arrived in what some of us still get to experience as free time, online and elsewhere. It is here, as we will see in this chapter, that digital capitalist culture displays its greatest ideological success; in other words, the spaces where work has, after all, become 'inseparable from non-work'.[30]

All this is not to say that self-commodification is an inescapable evil. In Tiqqun's *Preliminary Materials*, the mix tape postmodernism of their 'trash theory' presentation is at odds with the Frankfurt School hauteur (not to mention masculinism) of its conclusion: that Young-Girlification is a kind of extreme depoliticisation, where our explicitly feminised and narcissistic focus on self-curation has promoted docility and irredeemably broken with solidarity. Their only solution, disappointingly, is total rejection. Instead, we might posit alongside this history of self-commodification and the blurring of lines between work and non-work a history of resistance that reaches back just as far. Jane Fairfax, a character in Jane Austen's pioneering Young-Girl novel *Emma* (1816), when faced with the prospect of turning governess to ensure her survival, refuses acquaintances' talk of 'eligible situations' and her 'superior talents' entitling her to 'move in the first circle'. Instead, she describes the 'governess-trade' as the sale 'of human intellect'.[31] This is dynamite to the Young-Girl fiction those around her hold out as reconciliation – vicariously enjoying the leisure and status of wealthy people by approximating their appearance and sharing their space, a fiction that the novel knows elsewhere as the perpetual 'penance and mortification' of the life confined to raising (and fine-tuning the self-commodification of) rich people's daughters. In an otherwise arch-conservative text, while Jane accepts that she must perform femme class accomplishment to earn her bread, she refuses to have it sold back to her as its own reward. We've already seen Federici and Ptak exemplify the political gesture of making invisible work visible in housework and social media, and we might add to these the materially at least partially successful campaigns for sex worker's recognition to remedy the particular forms of exploitation afforded by hypocritical illegalisation and the ensuing lack of rights and protections. Most recently, we might add the struggle to challenge mainstream presentations of technologically assisted surrogacy; as Sophie Lewis has shown, surrogacy, while often waged work, is rendered hyperexploitative by requiring surrogates to act machinically as 'pure *techne*, uncreative muscle' on the one hand

and leaning on sexist ideology of feminine shame and feminine generosity to keep the workforce compliant on the
other.[32] Not unlike those latter-day Bartlebys of Chapter 2,
these workers would likely 'prefer not to' but have to anyway. In each case, they struggle not only for a wage, but to
have the wage relation acknowledged for what it is so that
they can refuse the Young-Girlification of work presented
as non-work. There evidently are strategies available for
some, albeit limited, de-Young-Girlification by communal
resistance, at least for some workers, some of the time.

Meanwhile, in as far as the Young-Girl subjectivities that digital capitalism affords us are concerned, it is
always worth remembering that there is no such thing as a
homogenous culture and there is no such thing as a culture
completely controlled by ideology, or even technology. As
we argued in Chapter 1, any prospective post-work society
would require nothing short of a thoroughgoing overhaul
of all values (so entrenched are our current ones in the
ideology of work), as well as new definitions of the 'care
of the self' and of human flourishing. We should admit
that many of those who might in some respects be considered representative Young-Girls, have contributed a great
deal to anticipating this kind of self-cultivation, and that
their invention of new forms of expertise, judgement, self-
experiment, and enjoyment may come in useful to us in
such a future. As such, we write in sympathy with the
Young-Girl and her relationship to technology. In 1981, a
decade before the internet and more than two before the

rise of social media, Donna Haraway's 'Cyborg Manifesto' engaged in the wager that the cyborg can stand as the figure-head of an ironic political myth that acknowledges two sides of the structural changes effected by 'the social relations of science and technology' in globalised, late twentieth-century capitalism. On the one hand, the cyborg stands for the 'informatics of domination', including increasing exploitation of 'feminized' labour ('flex time, part time, over time, no time').[33] On the other, it also stands for ways in which this new, networked reality of 'disrupted unities of high-tech culture' obstructs myths of origins and identi-tarianism deployed in patriarchal ideology:

> The cyborg ... has no truck with bisexuality, pre-oedipal symbiosis, unalienated labour, or other seductions of organic wholeness ... The cyborg is res-olutely committed to partiality, irony, intimacy and perversity. Unlike the hopes of Frankenstein's mon-ster, the cyborg does not expect its father to save it through a restoration of the garden; that is, through the fabrication of a heterosexual mate, through its completion in a finished whole, a city and a cosmos ... Perhaps this is why I want to see if cyborgs can subvert the apocalypse of returning to nuclear dust in the manic compulsion to name the Enemy.[34]

In the ambivalence of the cyborg, we recognise the Young-Girl. Like the cyborg, she stands for forms of work and life that have been rendered vulnerable to exploitation by their entanglement with techno-scientific capitalism, but also for forms of what Haraway calls 'emerging pleasures, experiences, and powers with serious potential for changing the rules of the game'. If much current evidence of online culture, as we will see in Chapter 4, is discouraging, the jury is still out on whether the intensification of online social life will ultimately lead to narcissistic self-annihilation or a revolution of our platforms and our economy that might render Tiqqun's description of the imperial Young-Girl unrecognisable to otherwise technically mediated futures.

## Amy or Peaches?

The process of Young-Girlification, where every aspect of our subjectivities and desires are increasingly 'put to work' can be registered in the difference in the public response to the deaths of two 'actual' young women in the years following the financial crash (Amy Winehouse was 27, Peaches Geldof, 25). Taken together, they offer a symptomatic story of the development of *lifework*. The particular intelligence of Winehouse's writing – set to modern hip hop jazz on *Frank* (2003), pastiche girl group soul on *Back to Black* (2006) – can be outlined with a brief comparison of two representative songs. In 'I Heard Love Is Blind', Winehouse's persona makes a series of excuses or attempts at reassurance to a boyfriend who she has drunkenly cheated on with another who resembles him.

The twist is that each attempt to diminish what happened inadvertently adds some torturous sexual detail: the very things that mitigate the crime for her are – we infer – only likely to be more heart-breaking for him. This song from *Frank* gets its reply on *Back to Black*, in 'You Know I'm No Good', in which sexual infidelity once again prompts a kind of misunderstanding between two people's desires. Again, the speaker's privileged sexual object is not the man, but the man – as it were – at one-remove (Winehouse wittily discouraged us from going through marriage first hand on *Frank*'s 'What Is It About Men?'). Thinking of the boyfriend while with the lover as in the earlier song, Winehouse's speaker can only reach climax with a composite figure of the body of the present man and the fantasy of the absent one. This time, however, the drama comes not from the boyfriend's presumed jealousy over the acts being described, but from his indifference.

This is an example of the sophistication of Winehouse's writing about desire that made her an artist wholly proper to the Young-Girl era. While Tiqqun wrote of an allegedly 'girlish' quality increasingly common to all of us, where no pleasure is experienced 'first hand', but is always somehow being performed for an imagined audience, Winehouse's songs were capsule impressions of everyday desire under such a regime. Even if at the same time, they said something about the mediated nature of desire as such: the unexpected ways in which our desires are always dependent on or appear unexpectedly in response to those of other people was something her Young-Girl art was able to be unusually articulate about. But this was only part of the story. As the footage collected in Asif Kapadia's documentary *Amy* (2015) reminds us, Winehouse's career unfurled during a high watermark for the old, openly feral British paparazzi, prior to its adoption of a veneer of restraint after the phone-hacking scandal and subsequent Leveson Inquiry.[35] For her five or so years of global fame, Winehouse's lifestyle and the accordant deterioration of her appearance, alongside her health, from alcohol, drug abuse, and bulimia was documented by crowds of photographers, until, in 2011, the removal of her dead body from her home in Camden Town was accorded, finally, the same treatment.

During these years, it became a cliché to observe that Winehouse's real life and her signature song 'Rehab' had come to double each other. Her 'work' of writing, her frequent inability to work when she turned up drunk to her own gigs, the *désœuvrement* of her collapsing body, and the 'putting to work' of every detail of her private life in the tabloids, coalesced in a single 'Young-Girl' object. But the footage accumulated in Kapadia's film presents another context. The documentary's use of archive footage made by Winehouse's family and friends makes it a record of twenty-seven years of transformations in home recording technology – from grainy analogue camcorders, to digital film, to early camera phones – but also of our changing use of such technology. As Kapadia reflected in

*Vogue*, there had been major changes in habits even in the few years since Winehouse died; the kinds of unguarded amateur footage produced for spontaneous amusement among Winehouse's friends had given way to a situation where 'you're filming yourself so that you can put it up on Instagram' and 'everyone films everything with the idea that it might one day be useful, or they're going to post it'.[36]

Like plenty of famous women, Winehouse was 'Young-Girlified' when every part of her life – from the physiological outward – was 'put to work' for the production of images, even if the fact that this took place mainly *off* social media makes her example already seem like it belongs to another world. At the same time, she was the author of a 'body of work', which while it often had overlaps with or played on facts of her life as a public figure, was also discrete from it. As such, her death could be mourned as the death of an artist, with tribute albums and cover versions, as well as an acknowledgement of a new poignancy of her music after her passing. But what then, of the death a few years later of another young woman celebrity, the sometime writer, sometime model, and general media personality, Peaches Geldof? When Geldof died following a heroin overdose in 2014, coverage in the British media was extensive, but was also cut through with an awkwardness not limited to the cynicism of the usual scoffers that the attention was undeserved. Undoubtedly plenty of people were sincerely saddened by this young woman's death, but what exactly were they mourning?

Unlike Winehouse or any other traditional artist, Geldof left no coherent 'work' on which other attendant kinds of audience identification could be hung. Rather, at the time of her death, her 'works' were precisely those of her personality and private life as such, performed across several social media platforms. As Diane Charlesworth puts it, Geldof's Twitter account in particular was characterised by its performance of 'good enough' celebrity motherhood – neither flawlessly aspirational, nor car-crash voyeuristic – which resonated with younger and working-class women. In discussions in the replies to her posts, Geldof's followers produced a 'collective dynamic that offered advice and shared information between members, not only in respect to Geldof'.[37] With such galvanising fauna of private life taking the place of a discrete creative achievement, we might say that Geldof's death was experienced as, if anything, *more* affecting for the absence of an autonomous 'work' which could live on in her place. When someone's whole work is their personality, it is difficult to take their death other than personally.[38] While the figure of the person 'famous for being famous' predates platform capitalism, the possibility of being so specifically on the basis of a constantly updated body of work charting one's daily life is clearly specific to it. Winehouse was subjected to – and to a great extent driven to death by – the imposition of the malign kind of 'Young-Girlification' Tiqqun warn against; but it was at the same time anchored by an autonomous work that was in itself a sceptical analysis of parts of our Young-Girl predicament. Geldof's work, by contrast, was all 'Young-Girl', and the transition and difference between these two highly mediatised deaths is one that is gradually being dealt out to the rest of us. Already, even Geldof's example seems rather quaint, at a time when the Kardashians have so expertly positioned themselves as what has been called the 'ideal promiscuous, entrepreneurial sharing subject ... both viral subject and viral object', distributing their everyday existence and ever-transmogrifying bodies over multiple platforms and media.[39] But rather than continuing to consider this as a celebrity phenomenon, we turn now to the ways the structure of the 'work' played out in the 'Young-Girl' deaths of these two women are actually representative of common experience.

## The hard work of being a Young-Girl

'I'm so lucky. I used to do this just for myself – now I can live off it!'[40]

This is a common line from the first generation of YouTubers to make substantial amounts of money from their activity on the platform. It sums up a story that was central to the mythology of internet fame in the early years of Web 2.0: a contributor to the video-sharing platform begins to post videos in their spare time; out of boredom, for fun, for free, for their own entertainment, for the interaction with other users and an experience of community.

They film themselves talking about their lives and interests: how-to tutorials, reviews, video gaming, fashion, comedy, politics, chronicles of personal crises and everyday life; one, some, or all of the above. Their followership reaches a certain level, and to their own surprise, they begin to reap revenue from the ads run before their posts. Some reach the point where this constitutes the equivalent of a viable or even a high salary. Other social media platforms, like Instagram and Twitter, have also brought careers to some who had visited and contributed to them for other reasons. They share a narrative of accidental fame, brought by initially uncalculated self-expression online, which then turns into work: the work of being yourself.

In YouTube's business model, based on monopolising and concentrating attention for advertising revenue, those contributors who make millions from their small cut of the company's profits are of course the exception. At the same time, the majority of those who become famous on social media understand very well and from the outset that they are selling a product.[41] Nonetheless, the myth of accidental internet fame remains powerful in a media format so centrally invested in the performance of intimacy. It also, we suggest, marks a notable moment in the history of the Young-Girl. At the start of this book, we noted Theodor Adorno's view of 'free time' as the dialectical flipside of labour, the bourgeois pretence of an 'oasis of unmediated life'. Adorno claimed that 1960s Americans had been trained to fetishise suntans, camping, and DIY, so that they were not tempted to use their free time to produce radical works of art or criticism that might challenge the mechanisms by which they sell their labour power.[42] Thus the hobby was seen as an invention of structured but strictly unproductive activity set apart from the world of work in order to sustain and legitimise it. Even if Adorno was right at the time to suggest that hobbies tamed unregulated free time threatening consumer society, and that free time as freedom was an illusion that kept workers obedient, it is remarkable that both of these forms of capitalist control are almost entirely dispensed with today. Critics have noted, from the 'netslave' volunteers of the early internet, to 'modders', who modify games online to the benefit of the gaming industry without personal gain, that forms of 'free labour' and 'playbour' are increasingly prevalent in the digital world.[43] In the myth of accidental fame, playbour is raised to the level of an ideal that is apparently opposite to Adorno's work time–hobby dialectic: that of free time play seamlessly turned career.

In this ideal case, labour has come to the hobbyist unbidden: digital acts of identification and performances of personality are apparently directly translated into popularity, which in turn appears to translate directly into money, a situation which then leads, apparently organically, to the requirement of repeated and professionalised performances to maintain both popularity and income. Self-assertion, via available technologies, becomes so inextricably intertwined with the current shape of the market in this scenario that differences between free time and labour time appear altogether insignificant. Central to this ideal is the appeal of the instant monetary reward for the likeable; an idea that, in the form of the good girl's reward, has long-established precedents. In one of the Brothers Grimm's nineteenth-century collection of traditional fairy tales, 'Goldmarie', a 'good and beautiful' girl is directly addressed by household tasks – loaves of bread cry to be taken out of the oven, ripe apples cry to be picked – and she performs them without question. Eventually, the girl is rewarded by a shower of gold coins that clings to her dress and marks out her double moral-domestic and economic goodness as 'the golden virgin' on her return home.[44] The old fantasy of gold from a quasi-divine nowhere for the good girl, of reward rather than wage as the superior form of remuneration finds its apotheosis and current form in social media stardom.

Yet there is a remarkable historical peculiarity. One of the strange, and apparently contradictory effects of the new technologies of internet fame has been that where free time and labour, popularity and remuneration seem so closely tied, they are also split to an unprecedented degree. One vlogger, Gaby Dunn, describes an experience increasingly common for 'mid-level web personalities' who are not in the top earnings bracket; these are people who have very substantial numbers of fans online, but do not provoke quite enough digital interest for this to translate to a living wage. These middling social media stars will frequently be recognised by excited fans but have to work in menial jobs to make ends meet, leading to awkward encounters at coffee chain and department store tills. As Dunn puts it, 'social media stars are too visible to have "real" jobs, but too broke not to'. It is difficult to assure an audience of your continued 'authenticity' when product placement is one of the main opportunities to supplement a social media star's income, and where any wrong judgement of the audience's taste is immediately punished by unfollowing.[45] The other side of the Goldmarie dream of spontaneous remuneration is only too apparent to independent creatives online: where money may suddenly materialise for the popular, it may as well not.

Once fame was only possible on the back of an infrastructure of record labels, broadcasting companies, film studios, and printed news media; gatekeepers who chose potential stars also shared the labour, the risks, and the benefits of propagating their work. The 'democratisation' of digital platforms for self-display have created an extraordinary excess of the labour of popularity, of voluntary, unwaged content produced in structural isolation that is monetised many times over by digital hardware and software providers, internet and electricity companies, the sellers and buyers of big data, platforms and advertisers, with only a minute share arriving, some of the time, with some of the content producers. Creative industries have long relied on precarious labour, and popularity was a volatile commodity before the invention of the internet. But the multiplicity of ways in which the agents of capital tap social labour online are remarkable. In 2000, Tiziana Terranova already argued that the internet facilitated an 'immediate valorization' of online activities at the 'interface with cultural and technical labour'.[46] Today, YouTube takes all of those who were once turned away at the casting, as well as those who just want to sing into their hairbrush, and makes money from them, and their audiences, quite independently and irrespective of whether they conceive of their relationship to the platform as work or play.[47]

In a sense, the myth of spontaneous remuneration is reversed, and shows its true colours, in this 'immediate valorization' of life by capital. The 'internet famous', who apparently turn free time play into money, but who in reality are compelled to fine-tune the affective labour of everyday popularity for very uncertain gain, can stand emblematically for the mechanisms of the 'gig economy', from task rabbit to Uber; celebrity itself has become a zero hours contract. YouTubers and podcasters on the one hand and taskers on the other have in common that they witness the total elimination of the social infrastructure of traditional employment: there are no regular salaries here, no pensions, no welfare, no rights, no colleagues, in sum: no job. If their valorisation is immediate, it is so in the sense of a lack of mediation by employment in the infrastructures of digital capitalism. Such a regime makes it easy to tap free labour, but makes it hard for its subjects to gain any purchase on a tangible opponent in a fight for working conditions, or even to find an audience for complaint. The hard work of the Young-Girl today, then, entails the digitally mediated performance of her life rendered immediately accessible to the extraction of value by digital capital, at a time when the structures and opportunities for waged labour recede.

The social media stars who do not know how to pay the rent, we might say, represent a development of the trend, from Amy to Peaches, of everyday celebrity. The most significant aspect of this everyday celebrity is that none of us are entirely exempt from it. Those of us who do not actively make a career out of social media are nonetheless increasingly compelled to present ourselves online in the same formats and according to the same rules. Facebook, with its billion users, is only the most obvious example of a platform that, with its focus on visual material and the 'like' button, trains its users to document and curate their lives for public judgement and approval.[48]

The celebrity principle, the social labour of popularity as the fundamental act of social interaction online is reinforced and normalised here; and even for the not-famous, it takes some unexpected, monetising forms. An early example was the use of social media to raise money for charity; the friend of a friend asking for donations to charity in their name as they run a marathon, climb Kilimanjaro or cycle across a desert is a familiar middle-class character from the first decade of the new millennium. But soon, personalised giving online became crowdfunding, as a number of platforms like Kickstarter offered the opportunity to ask for money to support creative projects and start-up businesses, and others like Justgiving made it possible to raise money for individuals struck by personal calamity or in need of expensive healthcare. Both types of funding have raised extraordinary amounts of money for causes that have captured interest and compassion online, but they also signal how unexceptional the idea of selling likeability for everyday survival has become. Where there are cuts to arts budgets, there is busking for support on Patreon; where there is no functioning public health care, there is convincing strangers that you deserve the money needed for life-saving operations. As Anne Helen Petersen points out, most crowdfunding for healthcare in the US, where it is an increasingly common practice, goes to 'faultless' diseases, like cancer, and not to ones regarded as 'blameworthy', like addiction and mental health problems.[49] Not everybody's despair is as fundable as Joey Rott's tragedy, a young father of triplets whose wife died in childbirth, and not everybody is able, like Kati McFarland, to draw attention to her condition, and her crowdfunding campaign, by articulately challenging her Republican senator about access to affordable health care in a televised debate.[50]

If private charity always tends towards liberalism and the reduction of the role of state-funded welfare, crowdfunding charity goes further in that it normalises habits of presenting basic individual needs as a sales-pitch that leaves no room for the articulations of rights and demands. It is worth noting here that while crowdfunding is often moralistic, it is not bound to any one moral agenda. Individual campaigns that seek funding for breast implants with borderline porn have proven as popular as those of the 'virtuous sick'. The common denominator is popularity, not moralism, and while the digital Goldmarie is required to do whatever work it takes in any one social digital context, her success is measured by monetised popularity alone. A UN Security Council meeting in 2017 provides an example of the flipside of this form of sympathy economy: speakers pointed out that 20 million people starving in East Africa had gone ignored by national and private donors, as only 6 per cent of the 2.1 billion dollars needed had been raised (as of 10 March 2017). It would seem that Africa was not Young-Girl enough; we increasingly desire the affective labour and performance of intimacy of the individual case that 20 million Africans are too abstract to deliver.[51] The cultural mechanics of the Young-Girl emerges here in another hauntingly global fashion; if we are victims of its forms of exploitation in our digital social lives, we also subject the rest of the world to its rules.

As we noted at the beginning of this chapter, we see the history of the Young-Girl as including forms of activity that accumulate wealth for capital without being recognised as labour, but also, and interdependently, as a genealogy of human desire bound up with capital. The most troubling aspect of the new forms of affective labour we have been discussing in this chapter, and the stumbling block to nearly all current analyses of games and toils in the twenty-first century is just that: that our desires are so effectively *put to work* by digital capitalism. Italian autonomist thinkers and French critical theory and its successors have become our most relied-on resources for articulating how late capitalism produces particular subjectivities; how we might stop producing them, a question that accelerates in urgency on the backdrop of financial crashes, digital automation, climate catastrophes, and the most recent implosions of the Western political consensus and the rise of the far right, has remained inconclusive. How do we get out of wanting 'self-valorization', the work of the good girl of capitalism?

In 1755, Jean-Jacques Rousseau, in his *Second Discourse*, argues that humankind's troubles started when primitive man, formerly independent and free, made the mistake of adding love and language to sex, and consequently developed a shared culture:

> As ideas and feelings succeeded one another, and hearts and minds were cultivated, the human race became more sociable, contacts increased, and bonds grew tighter. People developed the habit of gathering together in front of their huts or around

a large tree; song and dance, true children of love and leisure, became the entertainment, or rather the occupation, of the idle men and women thus flocked together. Each person began to gaze on the others and to want to be gazed upon himself, and what became to be prized was public esteem. Anyone who best sang or danced; he who was the most handsome, the strongest, the most skilful, or the most eloquent came to be the most highly regarded, and this was the first step toward inequality and also toward vice. These first preferences gave rise, on the one side, to vanity and scorn, and on the other, to shame and envy; and the ferment produced by these new leavens eventually led to concoctions ruinous to happiness and innocence.[52]

Here, Rousseau already acknowledges that leisure activity is an 'occupation', a form of work, and one that is bound up with the work of recognition and public esteem. Rousseau's image of an originary scramble for personal esteem is of course not equivalent to the later, Marxist idea of self-valorisation in capitalism, and neither can this Enlightenment thinker, even at his most pessimist, imagine that striving for fame might take place, as in today's algorithmic fight to the death for popularity, outside universally agreed markers of quality in discreet categories of music, dance, sport, and craft. Nonetheless, there is a sense in which Rousseau points to a sort of Neolithic Young-Girl at work at the origin of society itself, and in the same stroke, at the origin of all its miseries and inequalities. Rousseau proposes a clear line from purely functional sex to love, to architecture and family, to language and signification, to art and culture, to the social as the space of showing off and calculated self-display, to war and violence. We do not need to agree with Rousseau to see that his perspective usefully points to some intractable problems in discussions of human life and work. Rousseau's most important twentieth-century reader, Jacques Derrida, has shown that his work is pervaded by a double move that wants to pin down an innocent origin of the human just as it acknowledges how, from its beginnings, human life was already mediated by technology, language, and processes of articulation in the widest sense.[53] If we take into account this crucial philosophical achievement of the past century, the acknowledgement of the inextricable technicity of human life and work, and thus of the social, for our consideration of the Young-Girl, it becomes impossible to look to a place where we can take our desires 'offline' entirely, or even to an online utopia where 'multitudes' can engage with each other via technological artifices that are situated outside mediated power relations of some form.

We will take up this issue in terms of the question of the future of work in the next chapter. To conclude for now, acknowledging the originary technicity of the social might already help us to shift our perspective on some of the negative qualities generally attributed to the Young-Girl. If it is not such a long way from the stone age axe to make-up, and the unruly potential of desire is always mediated and channelled by technology in some way, it might help us focus our attention on how to rearticulate our social technologies instead of how to get rid of them.

# 4

# Three ways to want things after capitalism

We begin by taking up once more the text with which we closed the last chapter. Jean-Jacques Rousseau's *Second Discourse* starts with a remarkable account of the difficulty of writing about the past. Every thinker who has looked back to describe humans in *the state of nature*, prior to civilisation, Rousseau claims, has ended up attributing to the humans of the past behaviours and desires inferred from their own present moment of writing. Hobbes and La Rochefoucauld – the famous seventeenth-century cynics who Rousseau particularly criticises – thought they were demonstrating the inescapability of their own dark view of human nature by 'proving' man's original and natural barbaric tendencies. Actually, Rousseau says, their claims were misleadingly self-confirming, since the wicked behaviour they assumed existed in the past was only that of their own contemporaries projected backwards. 'All these philosophers ... constantly talking of need, greed, oppression, desires, and pride have imported into the state of nature ideas they had taken from society'. Whatever their other achievements of historical reconstruction, accounts of the 'state of nature' written before Rousseau's had – he claims – failed to historicise the human subject itself, which in its past forms is necessarily radically unknowable and impossible to recover: 'they talk of savage man and they depict civilized man'.[1]

In this analysis, Rousseau's rivals had acted rather like the Hanna-Barbera cartoon *The Flintstones*, which finds in prehistory the model modern family and suburban consumer tastes and habits of its own 1960s moment. For Rousseau, his rival philosophers were even ignoring the fact that – for all they knew – early man might actually have been radically good or virtuous. As such, what starts as an argument about the unknowability of the past quickly becomes one about the potentialities of the future. If it is plausible that today's 'bad desires' are merely contextual and acquired – not permanent and original – that means that they might be overcome, and our earlier good ones recovered; a wager at the heart of Rousseau's utopian political project elsewhere. Yet as Rousseau's commentators have noted, this framing of the discussion places him in a small quandary. For how can Rousseau presume to even speculate about the virtues of the human subject in its pre-lapsarian state when – according to his own criticisms of other thinkers – that state is defined by its untraversable, unknowable difference from us?[2] Rousseau claims to be eschewing the presumption of historical reconstruction and employing instead a self-consciously fictitious 'hypothetical and conditional reasoning'.[3] But how can such fictional speculation about the past be made from any other vantage point than that of the present, in all its ignorant modernity?[4] Rousseau is necessarily backed into his own inverted version of Hobbes's and La Rochefoucauld's 'Flintstones fallacy': presuming to speak of the virtues of the people of the past from the perspective of what constitutes desirable behaviour in the present. And since Rousseau also uses these claims to make projections about the people of the future, there is evidently a 'Jetsons fallacy' (after *The Flintstones'* sister show about a family-waged nuclear family set in a comfortably automated future). This fallacy would assume that the characters, identities, and desires of future people could be assessed according to those of the present, even if we assume everything else about life in the future to be different. E.P. Thompson remarked that the purpose of William Morris's utopian writings was to 'teach desire to desire, to desire better, to desire more, and above all to desire in a different way'.[5] But in the Jetsons fallacy, the desires of the present do not budge an inch.

In this chapter, we examine three variations on this problem in current ways of thinking about 'post-work'. We begin by extending our critique of anti-work authors from Chapter 1 to consider the other side of the tendency towards moral prescriptiveness we identified there; a version of utopia that seeks not to create new desires, but simply to fulfil the ones we already have. Second, we show how Silicon Valley's 'actually existing' post-capitalism is already based on an essentialising and static idea of what desire is. And finally, in a more positive development of the Jetsons fallacy, we speculate on what help anti-work discourse could find in the idea of organising a liberation project around our existing supposedly 'bad desires', which, contrary to Thompson's famous words, fail to transform themselves after all.

## The Jetsons fallacy in anti-work writing

In what we have seen is a founding contribution to the modern genre of 'post-work' utopianism, John Maynard Keynes articulates what might be seen as the real ethical content of all anti-work writing:

> For the first time since his creation man will be faced with his real, his permanent problem – how to use his freedom from pressing economic cares, how to occupy the leisure, which science and compound interest will have won for him, to live wisely and agreeably and well.[6]

This is quite a radical prospect. Keynes's claim is nothing less than that to live without work (or with much less work) will be to come face to face with our desire for the first time. There will be no more appealing to duty and necessity (nor pleading exhaustion): *we will have to do what we want to do.* Yet to call the question of *what it is we want to do* man's *'permanent* problem' is to inadvertently leave open the scandalous possibility that, not only has the problem always been with us, but that – being permanent – it will never be resolved. As it happens, this precise claim was simultaneously being made by Sigmund Freud in *Civilization and Its Discontents,* published a year before Keynes's essay in 1929. In virtually the sole reference to Soviet communism in his works, Freud remarks that whether or not the Soviets have the economics right, where they go wrong is in claiming that communism can ever result in everyone happily undertaking 'whatever work is necessary' and pursuing leisure the rest of the time in a state of peaceable harmony.[7] Freud's whole book grapples with the reason for this: the myriad ways in which desire precedes and exceeds its object and motive, and how easily it gets diverted, thwarted, harnessed, and bent into self-defeating shapes. This, for Freud, would be true in any human culture, whatever its choice of economic model and however much or little work there is to be done. Desire will remain the irresolvable 'permanent problem' of Keynes's overdetermined phrase, even when most of the ostensible material barriers to its satisfaction are removed.

Yet in a dilemma dating back at least to Rousseau, to write of the future requires that this problem is suppressed, at least on some level. Marx himself is explicitly suspicious of speculations about how we will live in the society communism was trying to bring about, but for two seemingly opposite reasons. First, revolutionary change that 'abolishes the present state of things' must begin with material 'premises now in existence', not far-off speculations; and second, the 'predetermined yardsticks' of bourgeois culture might narrow the horizons of the desirable in ways that preclude the possibilities of a revolutionary future.[8] Being explicit about the future is dangerous because such speculations are both insufficiently grounded in present needs *and* too meanly contained by them. For the anarchist feminist Emma Goldman, the Russian Revolution itself fell short on the grounds of the second complaint, precisely because its possibilities were too limited by pre-revolutionary culture. Leaving 'underlying ideas and values intact', it could produce 'only a superficial transformation'.[9] That the Jetsons must not be assumed to be living with the same desires and motivations, just with better and more equitably distributed gadgets, has often been treated as fundamental to any project of radical economic and cultural change. But as Kate Soper points out in her work on socialist utopia and desire, the impossible dimension of such thinking is that without 'some minimal continuity' between existing 'structures of needs' and those of the new society, it is hard to see where 'the emergence of the political will to revolution' could have occurred 'in the first place.'[10] Those radicals who will only concede that a revolution has taken place once there is no trace to be found of old institutions and affects, are left, says Soper, 'ask[ing] us to acknowledge that a certain form of society is an improvement on what it supplants while feigning ignorance of the kind of persons whose needs and desires it supposedly accommodates'.[11] On the other hand, any attempt to be concrete about the utopian future at all will end up promising to fulfil all sorts of desires from 'this side' of the end of work that may well have changed shape altogether by the time we are living in that society.

A fresh variation on this dilemma can be found in the simultaneously provocative, satirical, and perfectly sincere slogan, 'Fully Automated Luxury Communism' (FALC) and the version of the post-work utopia it invokes. In a short essay for *Vice* magazine in 2015, a few years before his manifesto of the same title, Aaron Bastani contrasts the future envisaged by the South African luxury goods mag-nate, Johann Rupert, with that proposed by the then-British Chancellor of the Exchequer, George Osborne. Osborne had just seen his extreme spending cuts approved by the electorate in the 2015 election and was seeking to extend these measures into a future of 'permanent austerity'. Rupert, by contrast, was worrying that the mass automa-tion and unemployment predicted by many economists would represent an existential crisis for his own luxury brands sector, as fewer and fewer people could afford to buy its products. Taking Rupert at his word, Bastani suggested, offered a way of moving beyond Osborne's austerity future, combining 'full automation' and the right to luxury consumption into 'the political adventure of our lifetime': one combining the familiar demand for liberation from work with 'Cartier for everyone, Montblanc for the masses and Chloe for all'.[12]

The dream of a post-scarcity future has often been invoked from positions of very great scarcity. Key to the rhetorical drift of Keynes's text is that it was written in a context where the arrival of such prosperity seemed very doubtful indeed, in the thick of the Great Depression. There is a subgenre of American folk songs about a post-work, post-scarcity world of 'cigarette trees', 'a lake of stew and of whiskey, too', in which 'the hens lay soft-boiled eggs', and 'there ain't no short-handled shovels', where the song's speaker himself is an impoverished hobo.[13] And as we saw in Chapter 1, the anti-work visions of the Italian autonomist and 'Wages for Housework' movements were devised in the context of economic crisis and the collapse of the post-war economic consensus. The present wave of anti-work writing – with the FALC slogan its metonym – has followed this pattern, conceived in the context of the recession following the 2008 global financial crisis and popularised among precarious young graduates.[14]

If anything, the habitual disparity between present famine and demanded feast in anti-work writing is even more pronounced in this latest wave, because it comes in the context of impending climate catastrophe. FALC'S enthusiasts are careful to play up the green credentials of 'post-scarcity' technologies such as 3D printing, robot workers, and lab-grown food, and to stress their potential as a remedy to today's inequitable and environmentally destructive global supply chains. But this does not quite do away with the sense of disjunction between, on the one hand, Bastani's demand for 'Cartier and Chloe for everyone', and on the other, an environmentalist discourse demanding 'de-growth' and a UN report declaring under-developed Cuba the only environmentally sustainable country in the world.[15]

In this context, FALC can also be seen as a *Verfremdungseffekt*-like attempt to upend public associations of the left with Stakhanovite self-discipline, dour ascetic piety, and mistrust of popular pleasures. Part of its rhetorical effectiveness is that it is difficult to object to without looking a little humourless oneself. FALC also takes a Gordian Knot approach to the 'theoretical incoherence' Soper identifies in Marx's refusal of concrete images of the future. In place of the feigned ignorance Soper describes Marxists imposing on themselves about which present needs and desires it is proper for socialism to satisfy, FALC meets us where our desire is in the here and now and promises to satisfy the lot. By brazenly proffering the bling of highly recognisable luxury brands, it also sidesteps the charge we made in Chapter 1, that anti-work writers want to liberate us from work, only to condemn us to their own sometimes rather worthy idea of a good time. But this commitment to luxury also requires a tactical projection into the future of desires that much radical thought has treated as specific to capitalism alone, and indeed has even sought to overcome.

To take a simple example: the hyper-realistic 'bleeding vegan burger' launched in 2018 would appear to be an exemplary proto-FALC product. As anyone who (like the present authors) became vegetarian in the 1990s will attest, traditional meat substitutes are reassuringly unconvincing. These new burgers, by contrast, seek as far as possible to recreate the texture of meat and even 'bleed' beetroot juice (says one online review, 'as a decade-long vegetarian, I was totally unsettled by the texture and could never eat this burger again'). We might even interpret the new realist fake meat as a trial run for the normalisation of lab-grown (and so virtually methane and cruelty free) 'real' meat.[16] It is becoming difficult to deny that veganism is an existential imperative: the planet simply cannot sustain animal farming on its current scale; and this, alongside greater visibility of factory farming's palpable cruelty, has led to an increase in people adopting vegan diets. Yet this trend has also coincided with the rise in the West of meat-centred 'paleo' diets (taken to baroque extremes by the culture warrior Jordan Peterson, who claims to subsist entirely on beef), and even an increase in the *meatiness* of meat products in popular cuisine: the ubiquitous pulled pork, hipster burgers ludicrously stacked like postmodern sculptures, and fries heaped with bacon.

A traditional response of cultural criticism would be to interrogate *why* this desire for meat should arise in the present context of ecological crisis. We might consult Roland Barthes on the relation between rare steak and nationalism from *Mythologies*, the critique of 'carno-phallogocentrism' by Jacques Derrida and within *écriture feminine*, or Carol J. Adams's *The Sexual Politics of Meat*: in short a whole canon of criticism on the symbolic violence accrued by our history of handling meat. The 'FALC' burger, by contrast, short-circuits this *cultural* critique of our desire for delicious but destructive things, using technology to cut straight to the *material* dimension of actual cruelty and environmental destruction, but leaving the desire itself intact. It is no more interested in the network of behaviours, attitudes, and oppressions that come with wanting to eat meat than Bastani is in our contextually specific reasons for wanting Cartier, Montblanc, and Chloe. An uncharitable reader might therefore interpret FALC as the extreme endpoint of Slavoj Žižek's account of neoliberalism's predilection for 'products deprived of their malignant properties: coffee without caffeine, cream without fat, beer without alcohol [...] warfare with no casualties (on our side of course)': communism without the need to renounce capitalism's selfish, violent, and sexist pleasures.[17] The more generous alternative is to see FALC as recognising the necessity of a radical withholding of judgement. Recognising the fact of desire's cultural-historical plasticity does not help us very much in predicting or predetermining conclusively which desires and which parts of desire are to be congenially met by the post-work utopia and which – like the vices of Rousseau's contemporaries – will fall by the wayside.

A second recent anti-work text, Nick Srnicek and Alex Williams's *Inventing the Future* (referred to in Chapter 1), also emphasises the need for the left to become the party of the plentiful future once more. While less unabashedly populist than Bastani, when Srnicek and Williams come to make their offer for what post-work life could be like, it is as if the very written genre itself forces them into the same problem of appearing to project the pre-existing desires of the present continuously into a future world:

> In such a society, the labour that remains will no longer be imposed upon us by an external force – by an employer or by the imperatives of survival. Work will become driven *by our own desires*, instead of by demands from outside [emphasis added].

The 'desire' Srnicek and Williams are invoking is the desire for meaningful human activity, rather than Bastani's luxury commodities. But a version of the same initial fallacy nonetheless applies. Bastani invokes the people of today as desiring fine watches and clothes, kept from them by invidious hierarchy that ought to be abolished (a move which requires him to side-line the question of whether those desires might be contingent on that hierarchy, as we have seen). More cautious as they are, Srnicek and

Williams's text nonetheless forces them to conjure a desire for meaningful activity, which also sounds a lot like it is simply *there*, pre-existing, unrealised only because of limits imposed by 'external force' and 'demands from outside'. As psychoanalysis has taught us, we will never be simply 'driven by our own desires', because our desires are never simply our own. There is always a certain 'outside' imposing on them and giving them their articulation.

This is a trap that, earlier in the book, Srnicek and Williams have explicitly tried to avoid with a sketch for a concept they call 'synthetic freedom':

> [Synthetic freedom] is constructed rather than natural, a collective historical achievement rather than the result of simply letting people be. Emancipation is thus not about detaching from the world and liberating a free soul, but instead a matter of constructing and cultivating the right attachments.

In 'synthetic freedom', 'we can experiment and build unconventional lives, choosing to foster our cultural, intellectual and physical sensibilities', while at the same time remaining 'open to whatever people might desire', in ways we have not yet been able to anticipate. In this part of their text, the authors are clearly off the hook as far as dehistoricising desire is concerned. They acknowledge that whatever freedom there can be, it will not be based on the pre-existing will of the 'detached' individuated subject, but will be highly plastic and contextual. Yet this formulation contains its own theoretical danger.

We have seen that the FALC prospect is a neat way of avoiding the tendency to prescriptive moralism we identified in post-work writing in Chapter 1. But if Bastani manages to leap out of this moralism, only to land feet-first in an under-examined 'liberationist' notion of desire that downplays its historical specificity, then, accordingly, Srnicek and Williams's attempts to bring nuance to the latter risks forcing them into the inverse manoeuvre. If there is no human essence that can determine the form the desires of the future are to take, then some kind of implicitly moralised 'outside' prescriptiveness turns out to be required after all ('constructing and cultivating *the right* attachments'). Sure enough, by the book's closing remarks, any unbuttoned 'luxury' in their version of 'Fully Automated Luxury Communism' has fallen by the wayside:

> Such a project demands a subjective transformation in the process – it potentiates the conditions for a broader transformation from the selfish individuals formed by capitalism to communal and creative forms of social expression.[18]

It is as if the discourse of post-work writing is condemned to oscillate between wanting to erase present desires on the one hand (here moralised as 'selfish' as opposed to 'communal and creative'), and to enthusiastically and uncritically satisfy them on the other. Later in this chapter, we attempt to show a way out of this problem. But first, what if there is already a self-described utopian approach to technology that claims to satisfy our desires without prescription in the here and now? What, that is, of the 'Fully Automated Luxury Capitalism' of today's digital platforms?

## What does Silicon Valley want?

One of the surprising things about Corey Pein's memoir of life among the overworked reserve army of struggling tech workers in San Francisco is the way that aspects of this neoliberal dystopia come to resemble a certain utopian 'post-capitalism' in themselves. At the top of the pile, programmers at high-end companies live a 'post-scarcity' existence every bit as luxuriant as those imagined by Fully Automated Luxury Communism. Accommodation, laundry, gyms, bikes, cafeterias, and booze are free ('at GitHub, they have a bar on every floor and a secret room with rare whiskies'), and steak dinners appear at employees' desks. Outside this charmed circle, struggling wannabes organise their social lives around the free bars of app launch after app launch – 'I don't know why I ever paid for alcohol!' – to which they are automatically directed by the Eventbrite app.

'It was much easier to launch a tech start-up if you could afford to always have food delivered and never had to deal with mundane chores such as doing laundry, washing dishes, or buying groceries', Pein reflects. Hence the techie joke: 'tech culture is focused on one question: what is my mother no longer doing for me?'[19] The apps and products these people create claim to identify and assist with problems 'we all' need solving. Their success appears to be based on honing in ever more closely on giving us everything that we have always wanted. But actually, it would be more accurate to say that what they do is universalise norms, desires, business practices, and prejudices (as well as workaholism and kinds of deskilling) that are particular to San Francisco's own weird outpost of late capitalism. This is 'literally' true of the way platform capitalism has provided an ideological figleaf and a model for increasingly insecure employment practices in the West since the financial crash.[20] But it is also true in a more figurative sense. Google buys its skilled employees twenty-dollar steaks in exchange for them working late, 'but with the extra time they've stayed at work, they've provided an extra two hundred dollars in value to their employer'.[21] Driven back to work in the morning in Wi-Fi equipped busses, these tech workers have everything given to them, on the condition that they leave 'work' as little as possible. What is this but an uncannily compressed version of the very bargain platform capitalism strikes with its customers, who get everything for free in exchange for *leaving the platform as little as possible*?

Our second 'way to want things after capitalism' concerns the role of desire in the quasi-'post-capitalist'[22] contracts the big digital platforms enter into with their users, which permit us access to this miraculous technology in exchange not for money, but for data. In one basic sense, what such platforms want is to know what we want. The aggregated data they collect and set their algorithms to navigate is always the record of a certain desire: an accumulated account of what has made people *inferred to be like us* click on what they've clicked on and do what they've done. Google's original monetisation of this technique by tying it to targeted advertising has revolutionised our entire infrastructure of culture, enabling users (and even other businesses, websites, and platforms) access to cutting-edge operating systems, communication technologies, maps, streamed entertainment, and more for the negligible cost of consenting to have these technologies constantly update their true owners on 'everything we do'.[23] 'The argument that data brokers use to defend such massive data collection', notes Nolen Gertz, 'is that they are trying to learn about us in order to *help us*, in order to provide us with better Google search queries, better Amazon recommendations, better Facebook news feeds'.[24] Yet they do so by adopting what Shoshana Zuboff refers to as the power to 'infer and deduce the thoughts, feelings, intentions, and interests of individuals and groups with an automated architecture that operates as a one-way mirror irrespective of a person's awareness, knowledge and consent'.[25] This is nothing short of a revolution in the archiving of desire, and of the use of technology to try to satisfy it.

Zuboff's phrase 'surveillance capitalism' accurately captures much of the agenda of this activity. But it also obscures the sense in which the platforms are not usually simply 'surveyors', watching us go about our business as if they were not there. Some 'always-on' systems such as Amazon's Echo do indeed 'survey' us in this passive and continuous way, while Google is travelling in that direction in its increasing harvesting of data when we are not using its sites or even logged into our devices. But digital companies in general are also highly motivated to *change* our behaviour. Not only in Pein's sense of making us dependent on their apps for tasks we used to perform for ourselves, but more generally in the way these companies are incentivised to find ways to get us to *be* on platforms for as much time as possible.[26] It is no wonder, then, that the arch capitalists at the top of these companies are among the most enthusiastic defenders of the idea of Universal Basic Income, if it means its recipients can spend more time at home on their devices.

As data-driven models expand into further areas of everyday life and governance, the legal, economic, ethical, and pragmatic ways in which these models are criticised balloon with them.[27] Our own point in this section is in some ways comparatively simple; or, at least, is focused on the complexity of the part of their operation that the architects of these platforms seem to have regarded as simple. The basic promise and the basis of the bargain made with these platforms is that their algorithms automatically give us what we want. But this idea of 'what we want' suffers by being based on a *pre-Freudian* theory of desire. Platform capitalism's algorithms assume that *we want what we want.*

Which is to say that it neglects the ways in which we can want things that may be absolutely intolerable to us.[28] You sit down to some concrete task only to get nowhere because of the constant interruption of Facebook notifications. You spend whole evenings in envy of some rival on Instagram. You resolve on an early night only to find yourself still online in the early hours. Anyone recognising these behaviours can attest that there is something within our desire that is perfectly willing to derive satisfaction from low-level destructiveness, from which we derive no conscious happiness and which we'd be embarrassed to share with others.

How else are we to interpret the familiar warning, 'don't Google your symptoms'?[29] Anybody who does so will be swiftly led to the auto-diagnosis of the most virulent and disabling diseases. Why has the algorithm learned to take us there? Why will we happily spend hours reading up on awful conditions we in all likelihood do not have? In such behaviour there is a self-confirming narcissism that takes satisfaction in 'knowing' the worst: and as far as Google is concerned, it is all the better, because these hours of winding ourselves up are also hours we spend willingly giving it our intimate data. Or, to take one of Gertz's examples, why are so few 'matches' on the dating app Tinder followed up by a message from either of the matched users? 'Such behavior suggests that users of Tinder are barely even engaged in casual flings. Instead it would appear that users of Tinder are *pursuing pursuing*':[30]

their pleasure tied far more to the thrill of the automated alert of the match than to any subsequent human interaction (even one mediated through the messaging function within the app). This is not, of course, to claim that such embarrassing behaviour started with or is caused by platform capitalism. The point is rather that tying so much of our cultural infrastructure to a technology predicated on delivering – apparently without mediation or judgement – on our desire, comes to look rather irresponsible when we remember that there are plenty of parts of our desire that do not need encouraging.

Platform capitalism is not the first economic system claiming to deliver maximum amounts of pleasure. In *The Ethics of Psychoanalysis* (Seminar 7, 1959–1960), Jacques Lacan suggests that Jeremy Bentham's utilitarian maxim 'the greatest good for the greatest number' crucially marks modernity's move from ideas of divine virtue to human pleasure as the ultimate social goal. Utilitarianism defined human pleasure as a self-evident and measurable good, and then demanded that everybody act in accordance with its decreed methods for achieving it. There is thus a certain standardising tyranny in this version of pleasure for the many. Lacan sees it at work in nineteenth-century industrialisation but also in the emerging social democracies of the time of his 1950s seminar. As imperial industrialised nations claimed to spread their benefits to their workers and to their colonies, so utility became an 'enchanting power' that hid its violence under the mantle of universal human pleasure.[31]

Today's tech innovators might happily agree that there was a violence in assuming like Bentham that 'we all want the same good', and even claim – in textbook neoliberal fashion – to have delivered us from utilitarianism's wrongly standardising idea of pleasure. After all, in platform capitalism, every individual user is offered options based on their own, singular behavioural histories. But to subscribe to this opposition would be an error. As Joan Copjec puts it in her reading of Lacan's seminar, utilitarianism's problem was never just that it assumed that everybody's pleasure was identical; rather it was that it could not 'conceive of a subject that would impede its own will';[32] and this is a conceptual shortcoming that platform capitalism has done nothing to overcome. That we habitually impede our own will is the most fundamental of Freudian discoveries. Human drives do not just appear in instinctual purity, but are, as Freud puts it, 'extraordinarily plastic'.[33] If, as was suggested in the previous section, this is true culturally and collectively between different epochs, then it is also true at the level of the individual subject, who endures ongoing internal struggles, her desires changing places, this one satisfied in compensation for that other, disappointed one. To design a system that automatically 'gives me what I want' shows a grave misunderstanding of what desire is.

Lacan's distinction between two different kinds of enjoyment in Seminar 7 is helpful here. On the one hand, there is the pleasure principle, which as Freud had already elaborated, does not mean the pursuit of some unbridled pleasure but rather the avoidance of excessive stimulation and 'unpleasure'. Its command, according to Lacan, is actually to 'enjoy as little as possible' – that is, just as much as is required to keep going, to get out of bed in the morning, to preserve our psychic status quo.[34] On the other hand, there is what Lacan calls jouissance, the kind of pleasure that goes beyond the pleasure principle, which he defines as a sort of stimulation that we are compelled to pursue but that is too intense to bring pleasure but rather brings pain (the pain of exceeding external frames of reference, of the norms we ourselves have internalised as the limits of the possible, or what Lacan calls the 'symbolic order').

But there is another way of looking at jouissance – not necessarily as our own destruction, but perhaps as the destruction of *our* status quo, psychologically as well as politically. Jouissance of this kind could even be regarded as a relatively ordinary, everyday occurrence. For Barthes, we find it in encounters with certain challenging forms of art, those which leave behind the 'mere' pleasure principle-like *plaisir* of having our expectations confirmed, and instead explode familiar codes into surprising and blissful forms of jouissance.[35] Alenka Zupančič, meanwhile, identifies jouissance with the pleasurable surprise elicited when we expect one thing and get another: a logic she defines as fundamental to the experience of falling in love:

> the funny side of a love encounter lies precisely in the fact that the other (that we encounter) is an

answer to none of our prayers and dreams, but, rather, the bearer of an unexpected surplus element that we might only get the chance to dream about in what follows.[36]

Certainly no one could rule out a momentary encounter with the spark of this 'unexpected surplus' emerging in interactions online, as it might anywhere. Dystopian accounts of algorithms controlling all our actions by reducing us to instantaneously placated zombies will not survive the innumerable occasions where what the algorithm offers up is anything but the answer to our 'prayers and dreams'. To take only the most banal examples, we are all familiar with comic instances of 'malgorithms', where the algorithm displays adverts wildly mismatched to the content we are viewing as a result of some superficial connection; or with the 'autocorrect fails' of our smart keyboards, which propose to insert idioms we happily use in one context, into ones where they are totally inappropriate. Our claim instead is that in defining and presuming to cater to 'what we want' in the way it does, platform capitalism's model of algorithm-navigated aggregated data tendentially gives priority to and even exaggerates the repetitive, conservative tendencies of the pleasure principle: even behaving as if 'what we want' could be limited to this one side of desire.[37]

To put it simply, a decision-making system premised upon inferring and incentivising future behaviour on the basis of a huge record of *what has gone before* is congenial to the repetitive logic of the pleasure principle because it has little basis (whatever its evangelists claim) for reckoning with the possibility that things will be different next time.[38] Scholars such as Safiya Umoja Noble are right to warn that algorithmic decision-making as currently organised is regressive, in the sense that it often replicates prejudices and disadvantages experienced by minority groups 'offline'.[39] But the model is also regressive in this more generalised sense: of assuming that 'what we want' can be anticipated on the basis of what we and others with similar data profiles to us have wanted before, in a process we could refer to as pathologically normalising. At the same time, there is a further twist required, because repetition is never simply replication, if for no other reason than because the repeated action is appearing in a context where the earlier iteration already exists. This means that every repetition produces a kind of remainder or residue, which itself gets added to the sum of what is being repeated in the next iteration. This might go some way to explaining why pleasure principle-led behaviours often end up taking such weird compulsive forms: either individually (nobody thinks they 'want' to spend all evening refreshing dating apps or message board pages, any more than they think they want to bite their nails) or collectively, at the level of what data 'learns' to produce for us (the 'bad virality' of extreme, disturbing, or just bizarre content online).[40]

But are not our complaints in this chapter about the repetitive, normalising impetus of new technology just the same as any number of performances of Romantic and technophobic *Kulturkritik* – defending spontaneous 'life' against deathly *techne* – of the past couple of centuries?[41] Or, worse, when we suggest that current digital technology's relentless offer of 'what we want' is problematic, are we not retreating into misanthropic territory, some 'heart of darkness' in human desire, one that only a deluded modern Prometheus would dare to activate? A simple historical comparison to our own argument would be the mid-Victorian anxiety over another allegedly too absorptive, too instantly gratifying, too repetitive technology: the popular novel. As the historian of reading Leah Price has pointed out, the nineteenth century was ambivalent about the practice of isolated novel-reading, celebrating it in some contexts, attacking it in others, in particular when it was performed by young women. As numerous fictions, conduct books, and satirical cartoons suggest, many Victorians regarded the compulsive reading of fiction as a cause of slovenliness among their servants, and (as in the great fictional example of Emma Bovary) as a source of neglect of conjugal expectations among their wives.[42] What is the difference between these – to modern eyes, quaint – fears and our critique of the too repetitive, too absorptive tendencies of digital platforms?

The fundamental difference is that whereas the old object of criticism was a form of desiring technology that certain groups by choice spent their time using (as has been true of any number of subsequent moral panics, over rock n roll, over 'video nasties', over computer games, even over some specifically digital subcultural activities like sexting or cyberbullying), platform capitalism is qualitatively different, because it concerns a technological dynamic we increasingly have no choice but to be part of. Algorithmically directed digital interactions are not merely one type of everyday behaviour among others. They are *the* model by which our most passive subliminal desires get amplified, put to work and fed back to us: and their structure and their assumptions about desire are getting rolled out in sector after sector in the lifework regime. As for the 'heart of darkness', the thing to grasp is that desire is not, in our assessment, some coiled spring 'released' and given form by technology. The point is that, since we are subjects whose desire is both changeable and sometimes motivated – in Copjec's words – to 'impede its own will', a technology that naively and automatically offers us 'what we want' will inevitably run into damaging contradictions. Suffice it to say, a fully automated society with robots directed by algorithmically navigated data would need to update its theory of desire before it started offering to rebuild the world in the image of what it infers about 'what we want'.

## Repurpose your desire

We might take the idea of compulsory desiring technologies further to suggest that, if digital capitalism strives to blur the boundary between work and non-work, it also strives to blur that between wanting and needing, desire and necessity. Who can say whether the self-employed creative, compulsively refreshing their Twitter notifications every ten seconds, is addicted to affirmation or dutifully managing 'their brand'? Or whether there really is a difference? In Chapter 3, we discussed how we are increasingly required to perform our desirability and the desirability of our lives as part of our work, and in the previous section of this chapter, we have seen how the online record of our own former desires are sold back to us in an algorithmically narrowing appeal to the pleasure principle. Digital capitalism harnesses what we want in ever more intricate and yet automated ways; perhaps this is part of the reason why desire has, at the same time, become a newly politicised topic of debate.

Two examples of cultural criticism from 2018 set the scene. In 'On Liking Women', Andrea Long Chu makes the provocative case that the gender experience of trans women like herself rests not on identity, but on desire; 'a matter not of who one is, but of what one wants'. As is the way of all desire, Chu argues, the desire at the heart of trans experience is unruly: not only is it painful and threatens to remain only partially fulfilled – 'your breasts may never come in, your voice may never pass, your parents may never call back' – but it is also likely to come into conflict with hard-and-fast political ideals. Chu points to the failure of the project of 1970s political lesbianism to excise desire for men as a matter of political principle, as well as to the conventional complaint some trans-exclusionary radical feminists make about trans women today: that they pursue just those bodily and stylistic signifiers of patriarchal femininity that feminism wanted to see abolished alongside the patriarchy itself. Instead of rejecting this complaint as simplistic, Chu insists, with knowing provocation, on the right to desire just those signifiers regardless of patriarchal implications. Making the point that desire generally arrives unbidden, her conclusion is that 'nothing good comes of forcing [it] to conform to political principle'.[43]

While she does not explicitly discuss it, Chu's intervention points to what a Lacanian understanding of the subject brings to the rhetorical battles around gender identity: if the work of desire makes us who we are, biology at birth cannot claim to be the ultimate determining factor. It is worth noting here that, as Chu herself suggests, the deployment of 'gender abolition' in contemporary hostilities against trans people (the absurd claim that the embrace of high femme style by the statistically insignificant number of trans women hinders the abolition of the patriarchy) tends to be merely 'a shell corporation for garden-variety moral disgust'. We might add that this disgust is ultimately founded in the paranoid defence of transcendental, quasi-racialised womanhood supposedly residing in biology; it would seem that for some quarters of feminism today, Simone de Beauvoir had it the wrong way round: 'one does not become, but rather is born a woman'.[44] But Chu's Antigone-like insistence on 'the force of desire' disarms biologism alongside the disingenuous variety of gender abolitionism. Like Lacan's psychoanalysis, Chu makes the definitive human experience not the satisfaction of needs, or unchangeable identity, but desire, necessarily painful and never totally fulfilled. In our identitarian culture, this has been inevitably controversial, but Chu elegantly shows that the case is defensible from the point of view of trans rights. As she points out elsewhere, 'as long as transgender medicine retains the alleviation of pain as its benchmark of success, it will reserve for itself, with a dictator's benevolence, the right to withhold care from those who want it'. This is once more modernity's standardising violence that, as we have seen in the previous section, Lacan identifies as lurking under the mantle of utilitarian pleasure for all. Against an idea of gender based on contented identity alone, which hazards that a person's continued suffering disqualifies their desire as inauthentic, Chu proposes the radical alternative of one that respects desire, and where 'the negative passions – grief, self-loathing, shame, regret – are as much a human right as universal health care, or food'.[45]

Partially in response to Chu, in an article titled 'Does Anyone Have the Right to Sex?' Amia Srinivasan pursues digital culture's sexual politics from campus shooters' online manifestos to the example of dating apps and sites. She points out how apparently innocuous 'personal preference' categories police romantic and sexual encounters to algorithmically reproduce the mechanisms of domination and exclusion inherent in misogyny, racism, ableism, and transphobia: 'personal preferences – NO DICKS, NO FEMS, NO FATS, NO BLACKS, NO ARABS, NO RICE, NO SPICE, MASC-FOR-MASC – are never just personal'. In the face of how digital culture cuts desire down to size, Srinivasan concludes that while there can never be an obligation to desire anyone in particular, there may be a 'duty to transfigure, as best we can, our desires'. The evidence for how individual desires are channelled and warped by pernicious but profitable hierarchical categories online indicates a problem Chu is less interested in: that while some desires establish themselves intransigently, others prove elastic – that while moralist preaching will not and ought not transform a singular desire fundamental to maintaining a sense of self (you cannot train yourself not to be trans), there are other desires, as we discussed in the previous section, that platform capitalism is perfectly capable of manoeuvring into increasingly limiting directions.[46]

The two contrasting positions can be productively mapped onto post-work writers' troubles with getting to the other side of capitalism: as we discussed above, to even want a different world we have to hold onto some fixed desires we trust will reach into the future, but at the same time, to hold open the horizon of radical change also requires the possibility of substantially changed desires.[47] Where post-work writers oscillate between promising to fulfil today's material desires and prescribing new ones, contemporary culture oscillates comparably between its attitudes to personal desire. While in both cases, the glimpsed horizon is a better world, the risk, equally, is moralism. As we will argue in this section, it is this second case of personal desire versus moralism, that points to another way to approach post-work utopianisms' problem with how to want things after capitalism. To return to the idea of transfiguring our personal desires: Srinivasan's example, taken from Lindy West's body positivity campaigning, of looking at photographs of people we find unattractive in an attempt to retrain and correct our personal desires and self image, does not seem a likely recipe for resolving the problem of the perpetuation and intensification of pre-existing social marginalisation in the form of 'sexual preference' categories online. Quite beside the fact that, even if it were possible, it is difficult to picture who might thank anyone for having actively re-targeted their desire at them (and plenty of marginalised groups already suffer from being reductively fetishised on the basis of the features of their marginality on dating sites), no personal desire-retraining can change the material and structural cultural basis of the oppression of marginalised groups. But material change can. And, as is particularly apparent in this case, material change is cultural change. To win the struggle for cooperative or public non-profit platforms, as is increasingly demanded by the digital left,[48] would be the first step: towards writing better code for our social lives online that, instead of keeping us there at the cost of addictive affective manipulation and reliably simplified pleasures, leaves more room for chance, for breaks, for the kind of surprise encounters currently edited out of our search results as well as our sexual preferences. Of course these new platforms could only show their full potential in a world where there is sufficient time outside work to pursue their pleasures, but their possibility demonstrates the point; if we do not want digital capitalism to put our desires to work, structural change, not individual retraining, is required.

On the level of the culture, rather than the individual, we might take Srinivasan's description of a 'duty to transfigure, as best we can, our desires' as a description of the changed mood of the 2010s in the globalised West. Molly Fischer describes how in American popular culture, 'a self-conscious moral duty in matters of identity, of inclusion and representation – had come to dominate discussions among creators, critics, and consumers alike'.[49] This 'Great Awokening' has meant, in the best cases, room for voices of under- and misrepresented groups to break new ground and develop new kinds of articulate everyday cultural criticism: in the worst, tokenistic inclusivity in unchanged formats, and a spiteful puritanism.[50] In the wider cultural debate, some of those unused to self-criticism have 'checked their privilege' graciously enough, others have made the most of what moralism always provides: a template for self-satisfied to-the-letter correctness that denies context and is wielded as a weapon to preserve the status quo.[51] However real and remarkable this new focus on cultural politics in all areas of life is, it also contains a warning about reducing political struggle to a cultural re-education that soon dwindles to the level of aesthetics. As presidential candidate Hillary Clinton told the crowd at a rally in early 2016: 'If we broke up the big banks tomorrow ... would that end racism? Would that end sexism?'[52] The assumption that economic reform is separable, or even an undesirable distraction, from combating racism and sexism sums up a version of 2010s culture in which an aesthetics of equality is substituted for the struggle for it.

Attempts to absorb deep structural inequality by cultural change alone, and a cultural change relying at times on simplistic moral dogma have not been very promising so far. These attempts suffer from what Wendy Brown has called 'wounded attachments': the fact that the gains imagined in a struggle against inequalities of gender, race, and sexuality are constrained by what is desirable *within* liberal capitalist culture – to the increasing exclusion of class from the debate, and with it the possibility of a much more ambitious challenge to structures of domination and exploitation.[53] Elsewhere, in the theoretical renaissance on the feminist left, the question of how personal desire meets capitalism and technology is addressed differently: the collective Laboria Cuboniks, in their manifesto *Xenofeminism: A Politics for Alienation*, outline a queer- and trans-inclusive communist feminism that takes its cues from Donna Haraway's cyborg feminism by beginning with our bodies' inextricable relationship to technology. As a 'technomaterialism', it aims to resist capitalist technoscience not by refusing its tainted means but by 'repurposing' them. The gesture is disarmingly simple: we know that this biotechnoculture has been bad for us, and that we are in many ways its products; therefore, 'absolute caution', as the manifesto puts it, is impossible, but resistance can begin with taking possession.[54] The aim, shared with other authors on the technologically oriented left already discussed in this book, is to directly challenge the ownership and control of the technological and scientific infrastructures of everyday life, and so combat no-alternative neoliberalism where it puts us to work in the most pervasive and yet often invisible ways.

It is this unfazedness by the extent to which we begin as bodies under and subjects of technologised capitalism, coupled with the belief that change is possible, that makes room for a different attitude to personal desire. Helen Hester, for example, a member of Laboria Cuboniks, takes the fact that women's bodies are routinely hybridised by technology (most prominently pharmacologically: by chemical contraception and other forms of hormonal regulation) as the basis for an activist gender abolitionism that, by embracing experimentation, is equivalent with a multiplication of possibility: 'xenofeminism is not a call for gender austerity, but for gender post-scarcity!'[55] Where the call is to 'let a hundred sexes bloom', there can be no room for the trans-exclusionary radical feminist complaint of the perpetuation of patriarchal gender ideals by trans people, or for that matter, any other ideological complaints about individual body modification. The overall goal to overcome gender as a system of domination is translated into an offer of creative bodily autonomy. 'Fully automated luxury communist gender proliferation', then, to adapt Bastani's phrase: with the same utopian charm of demanding everything for everyone. Here, the demand for women's rights also means the right for everyone to be a woman, or not, or anything else. What for Lacan is the ultimate ethics of psychoanalysis, 'not giving ground relative to your desire', here simply becomes an offer of autonomy as part of communist solidarity.[56]

Some new articulations of feminist socialist utopia, then, can accommodate what Chu calls 'the right to desire what is bad for you'.[57] Another way of putting this might be that, in this new feminism, there is a different confidence that meeting and supporting the individual where they are with their desires and needs in the present will not stand in the way of the struggle with technocapitalism. On the contrary, it can become its basis: take Sophie Lewis's work on surrogacy, for instance. She offers the slogan 'full surrogacy now' as 'an expression of solidarity with the evolving desires of gestational workers, from the point of view of a struggle against work'.[58] In her book, she advocates for the rights of commercial surrogates to have their highly controversial work better recognised as such, and to be better protected in the present; in the medium term, she makes the case for redefining their roles, for example to include continued contact to the children they have born where this is wanted; and in the long term, all this is considered with a view to a utopian future where surrogacy is not a commercial service but part of and model for kinship structures no longer fixated on reproduction but on mutual care beyond the family.

What, then, about what we have outlined as anti-work writing's characteristic problem, that when it proposes what we *might* do when we have successfully abolished capitalist labour, often ends up becoming prescriptive about the good life that could replace it? The simplest answer is political; if genuine democracy must be based on sharing resources, because only then can it be ensured that everyone gets fully and fairly included in decision-making, then achieving this will be enough, and the only question will be the one Peter Frase outlines in *Four Futures*: whether available resources and conditions will make it 'communism: equality and abundance' or 'socialism: equality and scarcity'.[59] This harbours a truth that often gets concealed when left politics are offered to voters: that ultimately, there is no getting to this better way of organising our politics, economy, and culture without a leap of faith. If people get to live in a way that frees them from wage-slavery and gives them genuine decision-making powers, who knows what decisions they will make about the shape of their cultures and who knows what they will do with their time. Post-capitalism's leap of faith must be that if systemic exploitation and alienation is replaced with a system that aims to give everyone access to what they need and freedom to do their own thing, it will turn out well. We will not end up with a war of all against all, but with something better than the world has seen so far. As far as desire is concerned, any vision of the future must of course address itself to what we most want right now – all the future is, until it happens, is present desire. But if visions of the future want to do justice to ideas of radical socialist democracy they would do well to be more confidently honest about the necessary gamble involved – that we do not know, and likely cannot imagine yet, many aspects of a future we nonetheless want to build – and accordingly to commit to the provisional, and to include as much room as possible for difference and idiosyncrasy in the prosthetic desires required to get us over the hurdle.

# Epilogue: share your limits

In this book we have looked at the ways capitalism puts our time, our subjectivities, our experiences, and our desires to work in unprecedented ways only possible on the basis of globalised technologies. The role of technology in human life has been ambivalent for socialist thinkers from the start. In a curious manuscript essay written in 1876, 'The Part Played by Labour in the Transition from Ape to Man', Friedrich Engels tries his hand at a historical materialist rewriting of evolution from the perspective of labour but gets caught up in the problem of technology. Engels takes the crucial evolutionary step from ape to human to be the development of a more dexterous human hand; he imagines how small and partial successes of proto-hands at employments that circumstances require have resulted, over the course of evolution, in the 'freeing' of the human hand – 'thus the hand is not only the organ of labour, *it is also the product of labour*.[1] Accordingly, there was labour before there was a human, and the human only came about once labour had turned her hand into a tool. Here Engels not only reinforces Marx's technological materialism, he also anticipates today's philosophers of technology of different political positions, like Bernard Stiegler, who sees technology and human species as inextricably co-evolving – 'the hand is the hand only in as far as it allows access to art, to artifice and to *tekhnē*'.[2]

Engels's own focus is on labour as such: he sees labour gathering early humans together to bring about language, better tools, the adoption of a complex diet, and the adaptation to different climates and locales, and finally, the development of agriculture, trade, industry, art, and science. But what Engels is most interested in is how human labour reorganises its environment with consequences that often cannot be foreseen and controlled. He is concerned with 'natural effects', like the desertification that follows the clearing of forests, as well as 'social effects', like the starvation of millions in the Irish Famine of 1847, when potatoes as principal crop fatally met the potato blight. Finally, he stumbles over the steam engine:

> The men who in the seventeenth and eighteenth centuries laboured to create the steam engine had no idea that they were preparing the instrument which more than any other was to revolutionise social relations throughout the world. [B]y concentrating

wealth in the hands of a minority and dispossessing a huge majority, this instrument was destined at first to give social and political domination to the bourgeoisie, but later, to give rise to a class struggle between bourgeoisie and proletariat which can end only in the overthrow of the bourgeoisie and the abolition of all class antagonisms.[3]

According to Engels's narrative, then, industrial capitalism is the product, however unintentional, of the evolution of human labour. There is some embarrassment in his quick announcement that this awkward stage is soon to be overcome by class struggle. The overwhelming impression at this point in the essay is that human labour and its tools – in other words, technology – have produced, as a natural outcome of evolution, the human species and capitalism both. Engels's overall outlook is determinedly hopeful; the point he is trying to make is that however explainable by labour's evolution, capitalism is the wrong use of the tools, atavistic in its lack of foresight and in its destructiveness of people and environment for immediate gain, a teenage humanity soon to be replaced by a more grown-up period in human history that will regulate the natural and social effects of human technologies in a way that will reflect a more sophisticated understanding that 'we, with flesh, blood and brain, belong to nature'.[4] And yet, once Engels has made the evolution of the human hand, as well as everything else that follows, the product of labour, it is difficult to shake the impression that, with Faustian inevitability, humans will be picked up by their steam engines' iron claws to engage in the destruction of their natural environment and themselves. Is industrial capitalism an aberration of human labour, or the inevitable development of its technologies? If historically, 'all higher forms of production led to the division of the population into different classes', can there be another way? The rest of his essay, before the manuscript ends abruptly and unfinished, is dedicated to more bleak images of short-sighted capitalist destruction, like that of the bare rock left behind by erosion following the burning of a mountain forest for one year's crop.[5]

Like Engels's narrative, the dominant mood of our time seems to oscillate between on the one hand a resigned acceptance of a catastrophically irreversible *anthropocene*, which – with the first human fire as the inauguration of man-made climate change – invites the thought that humans were always fated to destroy the habitable world; and on the other, the rejection of a *capitalocene*, where it is the insatiable demand for exponential economic growth that has got us to the brink of climate catastrophe.[6] Either way, the temptation lingers to regard technology as an evil and quasi-mythical force of destruction. And yet, Engels's idea of the human as a product of labour, rather than the other way round, also promises another way of looking at ourselves as technological beings. In the first instance, it opens up a way for decentring the human: there is no being human without technology; but equally, there is no being anything else without it either. As David Harvey points out, an anthill is no more natural than Manhattan; *tekhnē*, or artifice, engineering expertise or strategic rearrangement of matter, went into the making of both.[7] If, as living beings, we meet our environment through technology as our necessary prosthesis, then there can be no question of technology as an external force that we can succeed in taming, or escaping, absolutely. But it also means, by the same token, that it is not an alien inscrutable force. As Haraway confidently put it in 'Cyborg Manifesto':

> The machine is not an *it* to be animated, worshipped, and dominated. The machine is us, our processes, an aspect of our embodiment. We can be responsible for machines; *they* do not dominate and threaten us. We are responsible for boundaries; we are they.[8]

Machines do threaten us, of course, all the time. But as technology, they are provisional. And therefore we can adapt them, scrap them, reinvent them, as the individual case requires, and by doing so, change ourselves alongside our prostheses. No doubt many of our digital technologies deserve to be forgotten, or change to the point of becoming unrecognisable; in some cases, what seem like digital capitalism's excesses may end up being surprisingly useful in bringing about political change.

Even in their unreconstructed form, a generation of leftists has been using capitalist communication technologies for radical purposes. Since 2015, we have seen that it is the generation most naturalised to the 'bad satisfaction' of Web 2.0 analysed in Chapter 4 who have provided the campaigning base for a new wave of radical socialist parties and movements across Europe and the US. In the UK, Momentum, the left-wing campaign group founded to support Jeremy Corbyn's leadership of the Labour Party outside parliament, has found success by integrating left-wing politics into the most everyday social technologies of its young supporters: in viral comic videos, WhatsApp messages designed to be forwarded on to all one's contacts, a mobile app that has taken phone canvassing out of the organised phone bank and into the spare moments of the individual activist's day, and a 'My Nearest Marginal' and carpooling app, allowing activists to travel to where their contributions could make the most difference in an election. As Tiziana Terranova suggests, alternative uses of the technologies that are designed to subsume bodies under capital can work towards 'another machinic infrastructure of the common'.[9]

The example points to what is concealed behind the image of evil technology; not the malign and unstoppable engine of history, but the experience of political impotence in the face of the system that shapes our technological being in the malign ways it currently does. The way out of this impotence must be political, but our historical juncture is also an opportunity to make our changing experience of technological being central to political change. This opportunity, we argue, lies in seeing ourselves as the hybrid, prosthetic, provisional beings of technologies that we can change between us. If we are unfinished beings, connected to each other and the world by *tekhnē*, individualism makes no sense. We have discussed new feminist writing on the left that picks up Haraway's cyborg feminism – 'wary of holism, but needy for connection' – in its aim to turn technologised life towards anti-essentialist politics; we might add, once more, Jean-Luc Nancy's view that 'singular beings share their limits, share each other on their limits'.[10] The risk and the chance of a sense of self taking and changing shape where we are exposed to others and things, whether at the limit of our skins, our ideas, or of other modifying objects, might in itself be seen as our technical relation to life. As Derrida puts it, '*tekhnē* is perhaps always an invention of limits', but as Nancy insists, community is the experience of being unworked, interrupted, fragmented as we encounter them.[11]

'Share your limits', then, might be one slogan for a post-capitalist outlook on our technologies. In its spirit of connective interruption, we might take on the challenge to refigure our technologies, not only to minimise the climate catastrophe and redistribute resources, but also to give room for 'unworking' human encounters. In political terms, this might mean, instead of looking for harmony and broad brushstroke consensus, to look for the kind of creative 'democratic agonism' Chantal Mouffe proposes; in philosophical terms, the pursuit of what Jeremy Gilbert calls 'experimental anti-individualism' that resists 'the lure of conformist communitarianism'. In terms of work, it might just mean, that as we win the fight for technologies that free up time for all, we will gain more room for what Walter Benjamin sees as the essence of children's play: experimentation and openness to all comers to join.[12]

# Notes

## Preface: the putting to work of everything we do

1 Jonathan Crary, *24/7* (London: Verso, 2013), p. 45; emphasis added.
2 Theodor Adorno and Max Horkheimer, *The Culture Industry* (New York: Routledge, 1991), p. 189.

## 1 Lifework

1 See Keith Grint and Darren Nixon, *The Sociology of Work* (Cambridge: Polity, 2015), chpt. 3; a rare engagement with this tradition by anti-work writing has recently appeared in James A. Chamberlain's discussion of Nancy on *désœuvrement* in *Undoing Work, Rethinking Community: A Critique of the Social Function of Work* (Ithaca, NY: Cornell University Press, 2018), pp. 123–130, which shares some emphasis with the final section of this chapter.
2 Michel Foucault, *History of Madness: A History of Insanity in the Age of* Reason, ed. and trans. by Jean Khalfa and Jonathan Murphy (London: Routledge, 2009), p. 72.

3 Roy Porter, 'Foucault's Great Confinement', *History of the Human Sciences* 3 (1990) 47–54 (49).

4 Foucault, *History of Madness*, pp. xxxix, 536.

5 Maurice Blanchot, *The Space of Literature*, trans. Ann Smock (Lincoln, NE: University of Nebraska Press, 1982), pp. 171–173.

6 Richard Sennett, *The Corrosion of Character: The Personal Consequences of Work in the New Capitalism* (London: W.W. Norton & Company, 1998), chpt. 4.

7 For the history of the term, see Grint and Nixon, *The Sociology of Work*, chpt. 9.

8 Sennett, *The Corrosion of Character*, p. 72.

9 For examples, see Erik Brynjolfsson and Andrew McAfee, *The Second Machine Age: Work, Progress, and Prosperity in a Time of Brilliant Technologies* (London: Norton, 2014); Martin Ford, *The Rise of the Robots: Technology and the Threat of Mass Employment*; and with greater historical scope and accordant scepticism, John Urry, *What Is the Future?* (Cambridge: Polity, 2016).

10 Perry Anderson, *The Origins of Postmodernity* (London: Verso, 1998), p. 85.

11 Franco Moretti, *The Bourgeois: Between History and Literature* (London: Verso, 2013), pp. 21–22.

12 Richard Susskind and Daniel Susskind, *The Future of the Professions: How Technology Will Transform the Work of Human Experts* (Oxford: Oxford University Press, 2015).

13 Peter Fairbrother and Gavin Poynter, 'State Restructuring: Managerialism, Marketisation and the Implications for Labour', *Competition and Change* 5 (2001) 311–333 (319).

14 Forty per cent of Britons reportedly see their work this way; David Graeber, *Bullshit Jobs: A Theory* (London: Penguin, 2018).

15  Michael Hardt and Antonio Negri, *Multitude: War and Democracy in the Age of Empire* (London: Penguin, 2004), p. 109: 'immaterial labour, in other words, is today in the same position that industrial labour was 150 years ago, when it accounted for only a small fraction of global production and was concentrated in a small part of the world but nonetheless exerted hegemony over all other forms of production. Just as in that phase all forms of labour and society itself had to industrialise, today labour and society have to informationalize, become intelligent, become communicative, become affective'.

16  David Frayne, *The Refusal of Work: The Theory and Practice of Resistance to Work* (London: Zed Books, 2015), p. 40.

17  Figures from 2017 showed sixty children – mainly Muslim boys – being reported every week, often with no greater justification than having 'become overly passionate in some of their viewpoints' or appearing to be experiencing low self-esteem. As Karma Nabulsi describes, expressions of what are referred to as 'perceived grievances' with Western foreign policy are also to be reported, pathologising dissent and turning critical political engagement itself into 'an indicator – indeed evidence – of extremism'; 'Don't Go to the Doctor', *London Review of Books* 18/05/17 [https://www.lrb.co.uk/v39/n10/karma-nabulsi/dont-go-to-the-doctor].

18  'A Guide to the Hostile Environment: The Border Controls Dividing Our Communities – And How We Can Bring Them Down', *Liberty* (2018) [https://www.libertyhumanrights.org.uk/sites/default/files/HE%20web.pdf].

19  Chantal Mouffe, *For a Left Populism* (London: Verso, 2018), p. 36.

20  Chamberlain begins his *Undoing Work, Rethinking Community* with a similar comment on this work-centredness of radical politics at both ends of the political spectrum (pp. 1–2).

21 Andrea Komlosy, *Work: The Last 1000 Years* (London: Verso, 2018), p. 180.

22 Robert Castel, *From Manual Workers to Wage Labourers: Transformation of the Social Question*, trans. Richard Boyd (New Brunswick, NJ: Transaction Publishers, 2003), p. xiii.

23 Guy Standing, *Work after Globalization: Building Occupational Citizenship* (Northampton, MA: Edward Elgar, 2009), p. 43.

24 William Beveridge quoted in David Kynaston, *Austerity Britain, 1945–51* (London: Bloomsbury, 2007), p. 26.

25 Nancy Fraser, 'Contradictions of Capital and Care', *New Left Review* 100 (2016) 99–117 (111).

26 Mariarosa Dalla Costa and Selma James, *The Power of Women and the Subversion of Community* (Bristol: Falling Wall Press, 1975), p. 26.

27 Angela Davis, *Women, Race and Class* (London: The Women's Press, 1981), pp. 13–14.

28 Shulamith Firestone, *The Dialectic of Sex: The Case for Feminist Revolution* (London: Verso, 2015), p. 105.

29 Ira Katznelson, *When Affirmative Action Was White: An Untold History of Racial Inequality in Twentieth-Century America* (New York: Norton, 2005), pp. 142–143; also, Jill Quadagno, *The Colour of Welfare: How Racism Undermined the War on Poverty* (Oxford: Oxford University Press, 1994).

30 Isabel Lorey, *State of Insecurity: Government of the Precarious*, trans. Aileen Derieg (London: Verso, 2015), p. 42.

31 See J.A. Smith, 'Fake News Literary Criticism' in *Brexit and Literature: Critical and Cultural Responses*, ed. by Robert Eaglestone (London: Routledge, 2018), pp. 118–130.

32 Quoted in Anton Jäger, 'Why "Post-Work" Doesn't Work', *Jacobin* 19/11/18 [https://www.jacobinmag.com/2018/11/post-work-ubi-nick-srnicek-alex-williams].

33  Franco 'Bifo' Berardi, praised in Mark Fisher, *K-Punk: The Collected and Unpublished Writings*, ed. by Darren Ambrose (London: Repeater, 2018), pp. 769–770.

34  Andy Beckett, *When the Lights Go Out: What Really Happened to Britain in the Seventies* (London: Faber and Faber, 2009), pp. 143–144.

35  Peter Frase, *Four Futures: Life after Capitalism* (London: Verso, 2016), p. 43.

36  See Smith, 'Fake News Literary Criticism' on the examples of Richard Hoggart's *The Uses of Literacy* (1957) and F.R. Leavis's writings of the 1960s, collected as *Nor Shall My Sword* (1972).

37  Frayne, *The Refusal of Work*, p. 83; for interim contributions, see, for example, Jeremy Rifkin, *The End of Work* (New York: Putnam Books, 1997); and Stanley Aronowitz and Jonathan Cutler (eds.), *Post-Work: The Wages of Cybernation* (New York: Routledge, 1998).

38  Frederick Harry Pitts, 'Beyond the Fragment: Postoperaismo, Postcapitalism and Marx's "Notes on Machines", 45 Years On', *Economy and Society* 46:3–4 (2017) 324–345.

39  William Mitchell and Thomas Fazi, *Reclaiming the State: A Progressive Vision for a Post-Neoliberal World* (London: Pluto, 2017), chpt. 9.

40  On the necessity of separating the philosophical dimension of the question in this way, see John Danaher, 'Will Life Be Worth Living in a World Without Work? Technological Unemployment and the Meaning of Life', *Science and Engineering Ethics* 23:1 (2017) 41–64.

41  Frayne, *The Refusal of Work*, p. 158.

42  André Gorz, *Reclaiming Work: Beyond the Wage Based Society* (Cambridge: Polity, 1999), p. 113.

43  Frayne, *The Refusal of Work*, p. 180; and elsewhere: 'people were motivated by a sense of genuine utility: a desire to create, help others, and avoid ethically dubious work. They defined success not in terms of material wealth or social status but in terms of the opportunity to develop their personal capacities ... Some used their time to take care of their elderly parents or play with their children' (p. 155).

44  Virginia Woolf, *A Room of One's Own and Three Guineas*, ed. by Anna Snaith (Oxford: Oxford University Press), p. 143.

45  Q.D. Leavis, 'Caterpillars of the Commonwealth Unite!', *Scrutiny* 7 (1938) 203–214.

46  In a remarkably precise inversion of Leavis's gender conservatism and class radicalism, when Woolf was advised (by the founder of the Fabian Society, Beatrice Webb) to treat her marriage only as a 'waste paper basket of the emotions' to clear her mind for her art, her retort was, 'I daresay an old family servant would do as well'; Leonard Woolf, *Beginning Again: An Autobiography of the Years 1911 to 1918* (London: The Hogarth Press, 1964), p. 117.

47  Frayne, *The Refusal of Work*, p. 40.

48  Frase, *Four Futures*, pp. 46–47; Nick Srnicek and Alex Williams, *Inventing the Future: Postcapitalism and a World without Work* (London: Verso, 2015), pp. 113–114; Helen Hester, *Xenofeminism* (Cambridge: Polity, 2018), chpt. 1; Sophie Lewis, *Full Surrogacy Now: Feminism Against Family* (London: Verso, 2019).

49  Srnicek and Williams, *Inventing the Future*, pp. 113–114.

50  Karl Marx, *The German Ideology*, trans. by W. Lough, C. Dutt and C.P. Magill (London: Lawrence and Wishart, 1970), p. 54; for contextualisation in Marx's wider work, see Frase, *Four Futures*, pp. 38–41.

51  Kathi Weeks, *The Problem with Work: Feminism, Marxism, Antiwork Politics and Postwork Imaginaries* (Durham, NC: Duke University Press, 2011), pp. 204, 209.

52  Erich Fromm, *Marx's Concept of Man* (London: Continuum, 2003), p. 50.

53  Srnicek and Williams, *Inventing the Future*, p. 85.

54  Frayne, *The Refusal of Work*, p. 36.

55  Owen Hatherley, 'Work and Non-Work', *Libcom* 22/04/13 [https://libcom.org/library/work-non-work-owen-hatherley].

56  Jean-Luc Nancy, *The Inoperative Community*, trans. by Peter Connor, Lisa Garbus, Michael Holland, and Simona Sawhney (Minneapolis, MN: University of Minnesota Press, 1991), p. 2.

57  William Empson, *Some Versions of the Pastoral* (London: Penguin, 1995 [1935]), p. 20.

58  Nancy, *Inoperative Community*, p. 3.

59  Nancy, *Inoperative Community*, p. 7.

60  Donald E. Pizer (ed.), *American Communal Utopias* (Chapel Hill, NC: University of North Carolina Press, 1997).

61  Nancy, *Inoperative Community*, p. 4.

62  Nancy, *Being Singular Plural*, trans. by Robert D. Richardson and Anne E. O'Byrne (Stanford, CA: Stanford University Press, 2000), p. 66.

63  Nancy, *Inoperative Community*, p. 28.

64  Raymond Williams, 'The Bloomsbury Fraction', *Culture and Materialism* (London: Verso, 2005), pp. 148–169.

65  Nancy, *Inoperative Community*, p. 41; it is for this reason that Jeremy Gilbert includes Nancy among the thinkers of what he calls 'the non-fascist crowd': the communal that does not demand the destruction of the individual, in *Common Ground: Democracy and Collectivity in an Age of Individualism* (London: Pluto, 2014), chpt. 5.

66 'A singular being has the precise structure of a being of writing: it resides only in communication'. Nancy, *Inoperative Community*, p. 78.

67 Nancy, *Inoperative Community*, p. 29.

68 Nancy, *Inoperative Community*, p. 78.

69 Jacques Derrida, *Of Grammatology*, trans by Gayatari Chakravorty Spivak (Baltimore, MD: The John Hopkins University Press), p. 158.

## 2 Work expulsions

1 See Christopher Ricks, *T.S. Eliot and Prejudice* (Berkeley, LA: University of California Press, 1988), chpt. 1.

2 Walter Benjamin, 'Franz Kafka: On the Tenth Anniversary of His Death' in *Selected Writings*, ed. by Michael W. Jennings and others (Cambridge, MA: The Belknap Press, 2005), v. 2, p. 796.

3 Thanks to Sue Tilley for confirming these details.

4 In Nancy Fraser, *Fortunes of Feminism: From State Managed Capitalism to Neoliberal Crisis* (London: Verso, 2013), pp. 89, 94; also, Ruth Levitas, *The Inclusive Society: Social Exclusion and New Labour* (Basingstoke: Palgrave, 2005), p. 15.

5 Adam Perkins, *The Welfare Trait* (London: Palgrave, 2015).

6 This is not to minimise the significance of the changes they did effect. For an account of the experience of unemployment and new limitations on unemployment benefit, as well as organised resistance to them, see Brian Marren, *We Shall Not Be Moved: How Liverpool's Working Class Fought Redundancies, Closures and Cuts in the Age of Thatcher* (Manchester: Manchester University Press, 2016), chpt. 4.

7  Social Justice Policy Group, *Breakthrough Britain: Ending the Costs of Social Breakdown* (London: Social Justice Policy Group, 2007), p. 215; intriguingly, the framing of this right-wing text that supplied the blueprint for the 2010 Coalition government's reforms is one of declining conditionality of benefits from the proposals of 1942 until 1985. In its authors' framing, 1996 marked the start of an attempt to 'reintroduce conditionality'.

8  Gerry Mooney and Alex Law, 'New Labour, "Modernisation" and Welfare Worker Resistance' in *New Labour/Hard Labour?: Restructuring and Resistance Inside the Welfare Industry*, ed. by Gerry Mooney and Alex Law (Bristol: The Policy Press, 2007), 1–22 (p. 4).

9  Stuart Hall, *Selected Politics Writings: The Great Moving Right Show and Other Essays*, ed. by Sally Davison, David Featherstone, Michael Rustin and Bill Schwarz (London: Lawrence and Wishart, 2017), p. 288.

10  Andrew Wallace, *Remaking Community?: New Labour and the Governance of Poor Neighbourhoods* (Farnham: Ashgate, 2010), p. 23; Levitas, *The Inclusive Society*, p. 191.

11  Levitas, *The Inclusive Society*, p. 11.

12  Frank Field MP, 'Britain's Underclass: Countering the Growth' in *Charles Murray and the Underclass: The Developing Debate*, ed. by David G. Green (London: IEA, 1996), pp. 57–60 (p. 57): 'his errors of fact, or unusualness of interpretation should not blind anyone to Murray's main message'.

13  Richard Seymour, *Corbyn: The Strange Rebirth of Radical Politics* (London: Verso, 2016), p. 155.

14  Richard Power Sayeed, *1997: The Future That Never Happened* (London: Zed Books, 2017); looking back on the occasion of Blair's departure as Prime Minister, Blairite intellectual Anthony Giddens (on whom more below)

conceded that 'Labour has been coy about its egalitarian aspirations, couching them in the vague language of social exclusion', with the effect that 'one could be forgiven for doubting the strength' of its commitment to social justice; *Over to You Mr Brown: How Labour Can Win Again* (Cambridge: Polity, 2007), p. 28.

15  Peter Mandelson, *Labour's Next Steps: Tackling Social Exclusion* (London: Fabian Society, 1997), p. 35.

16  Alex Callinicos, 'Social Theory Put to the Test of Politics: Pierre Bourdieu and Anthony Giddens', *New Left Review* 1:236 (1999), 77–102 (86–87).

17  Anthony Giddens, *Modernity and Self-Identity: Self and Society in the Late Modern Age* (Cambridge: Polity, 1991), p. 81.

18  David Harvey, *A Brief History of Neoliberalism* (Oxford: Oxford University Press, 2005), p. 69.

19  Wallace, *Remaking Community?*, p. 20.

20  Tom Slater, 'The Myth of "Broken Britain": Welfare Reform and the Production of Ignorance', *Antipode* 46:4 (2012) 948–968 (956).

21  Giddens, *Modernity and Self-Identity*, p. 129.

22  Andreas Cebulla, Karl Ashworth, David Greenberg, and Robert Walker, *Welfare-to-Work: New Labour and the US Experience* (Aldershot: Ashgate, 2005), p. 4.

23  Ivor Southwood, *Non-Stop Inertia* (Winchester: Zero, 2011), p. 49.

24  On 'work-for-labour' see Guy Standing, 'Understanding the Precariat through Labour and Work', *Development and Change* 45:5 (2014) 956–980 (963).

25  Slater, 'The Myth of "Broken Britain"' 660.

26  For comment on the connection between online platforms and precarious labour, see J.A. Smith, *Other People's Politics: Populism to Corbynism* (Winchester: Zero, 2020), pp. 17–18.

27  Although as one piece covering the crime observed, Beasley
    underestimated the kinds of surrogate intimacies formed
    under conditions of economic and familial breakdown
    between the men he appealed to; 'old high-school friends
    who chat so many times a day that they need to buy
    themselves walkie-talkies; a father who texts his almost-
    grown sons as he goes to bed at night and as he wakes up in
    the morning' (Hanna Rosin, 'Murder by Craigslist', *The
    Atlantic* 09/13 [https://www.theatlantic.com/magazine/
    archive/2013/09/advertisement-for-murder/309435]).

28  Russ Castronovo, 'Occupy Bartleby', *J19: The Journal of
    Nineteenth-Century Americanists* 2:2 (2014) 253–272.

29  Charles Dickens, *Martin Chuzzlewit*, ed. by P.N. Furbank
    (London: Penguin, 1968), p. 681.

30  Arthur Conan Doyle, *Sherlock Holmes: The Complete
    Illustrated Short Stories* (London: Chancellor Press, 1985,
    pp. 210, 31, 156.

31  Bram Stoker, *Dracula* (London: HarperCollins, 2011), p. 17.

32  Henry James, *The Turn of the Screw* (New York: Norton,
    1999), p. 6.

33  See, for example, Alexander Cooke, 'Resistance, Potentiality
    and the Law: Deleuze and Agamben on "Bartleby"', *Angelaki:
    Journal of the Theoretical Humanities* 10:3 (2005) 79–89.

34  Southwood, *Non-Stop Inertia*, p. 79.

35  The latter irony noted in Andrew Knighton, 'The Bartleby
    Industry and Bartleby's Idleness', *ESQ: A Journal of the
    American Renaissance* 53:2 (2007) 184–215.

36  Allen Clarke, *The Effects of the Factory System* (London: Grant
    Richards, 1899), pp. 51–52, 32.

37  Philip Alston, 'Statement on Visit to the United Kingdom'
    (2018) [https://www.ohchr.org/en/NewsEvents/Pages/
    DisplayNews.aspx?NewsID=23881&LangID=E].

38 Danny Dorling, 'Short Cuts', *London Review of Books* 39:22 (2017) [https://www.lrb.co.uk/v39/n22/danny-dorling/short-cuts].

39 Jason Heyes, Mark Tomlinson, and Adam White, 'Underemployment and Well-Being in the UK before and after the Great Recession', *Work, Employment and Society* 31:1 (2017) 71–89 (85).

40 Frayne, *The Refusal of Work*, p. 38.

41 Jamie Woodcock, *Working the Phones: Control and Resistance in Call Centres* (London: Pluto, 2017), pp. 71–72.

42 Frayne, *The Refusal of Work*, p. 148.

43 Nic Murray, 'No Crying in the Breakroom' in *The W ork Cure: Critical Essays on Work and Wellness*, ed. by David Frayne (Monmouth: PCC Books, 2019), pp. 45–60 (p. 53).

44 Quoted in Tim Bale, *The Conservative Party: From Thatcher to Cameron* (Cambridge: Polity, 2010), p. 146; for a gossipy account of the internal forces involved in the direction of Coalition welfare policy, see Matthew D'Ancona, *In It Together: The Inside Story of the Coalition Government* (London: Penguin, 2013), chpt. 8.

45 Alex Hern, 'Tesco's Unpaid Labour Shows the Flaw at the Heart of Workfare', *Left Foot Forward* 16/02/12 [https://leftfootforward.org/2012/02/tescos-unpaid-labour-shows-the-flaw-at-the-heart-of-workfare]; Ewa Jasiewicz, 'Poverty Pay Is No Alternative to Workfare: Why We're Telling Sainsbury's to Pay Up', *Red Pepper* 01/07/12 [https://www.redpepper.org.uk/poverty-pay-workfare]; Martin Dunne, 'My Job Was Replaced by a Workfare Placement', *Guardian* 03/03/12 [https://www.theguardian.com/commentisfree/2012/mar/03/job-replaced-workfare-placement].

46 Patrick Butler, 'Shelter Warns of Leap in Working Homeless as Families Struggle', *Guardian* 23/07/18 [https://www.theguardian.com/society/2018/jul/23/shelter-warns-of-leap-in-working-homeless-as-families-struggle].

47 Michael Adler, 'A New Leviathan: Benefit Sanctions in the Twenty-first Century', *Journal of Law and Society* 43:2 (2016) 195–227 (201–202).

48 '4 Out of 10 PIP Claimants Do Not Appeal as It Would Be Too Stressful', *Disability Rights UK* 10/09/18 [https://www.disabilityrightsuk.org/news/2018/september/4-out-10-pip-claimants-do-not-appeal-it-would-be-too-stressful].

49 Ivor Southwood, 'The Black Dog' in *The Work Cure: Critical Essays on Work and Wellness*, ed. by David Frayne (Monmouth: PCC Books, 2019), pp. 29–44 (p. 39).

50 Alston, 'Statement on Visit to the United Kingdom'.

51 Del Roy Fletcher and Sharon Wright, 'A Hand Up or a Slap Down?: Criminalising Benefit Claimants in Britain via Strategies of Surveillance, Sanctions and Deterrence', *Critical Social Policy* 38:2 (2017) 323–344 (344).

52 'The main effect of imposing sanctions is to eject claimants from the benefits system and to further distance them from the world of work'; Adler, 'A New Leviathan' 219.

53 Saskia Sassen, *Expulsions: Brutality and Complexity in the Global Economy* (Cambridge, MA: The Belknap Press, 2014), p. 36.

54 See also Andrew Gibson, *Modernity and the Political Fix* (London: Bloomsbury, 2019), p. 3.

55 [International Labour Organisation], *Women and Men in the Informal Economy: A Statistical Picture. Third Edition* (2018) [https://www.ilo.org/wcmsp5/groups/public/---dgreports/---dcomm/documents/publication/wcms_626831.pdf]; the scholar of 'footloose' labour in the Third World, Jan Breman, usefully summarises a growing

interchangeability of 'formal' and 'informal' employment which will seem familiar after the analysis given here: 'A vast number of workers are employed in informal conditions within the formal economy, through outsourcing and subcontracting. "Informality" here is simply a way to cheapen the price of labour, to reduce it to a pure commodity, with no provisions for security or sustainable working conditions, let alone for protection against adversity. You buy labour but only for as long as you need it; then you get rid of it again. That is very much the way of the informal economy. Another important reason why the informal economy is so popular among the employers and owners of capital – not to mention the IMF and World Bank – is because it makes collective action very difficult: the workforce is floating, so it's very hard to organise. If you sell your labour power standing in the morning market for the day, how can you engage in collective action with those around you, with your competitors?'; 'Interview: A Footloose Scholar', *New Left Review* 94 (2015) 45–75 (57–58).

## 3 We Young-Girls

1   Laurel Ptak, 'Wages for Facebook' [http://wagesforfacebook.com].

2   Christian Fuchs, *Digital Labour and Karl Marx* (New York: Routledge, 2014), p. 248; for a round-up of associated neologisms and the adoption of these terms within scholarship, see Richard Heeks, 'Digital Economy and Digital Labour Terminology', Centre for Development Informatics, working paper 70 (2017).

3   Nick Srnicek, *Platform Capitalism* (Cambridge: Polity, 2017), p. 54.

4   Silvia Federici, *Wages Against Housework* (Bristol: Falling Walls Press and Power of Women Collective, 1975).

5   This has been noted since in more general terms by scholars like Kylie Jarrett, who suggests that 'the forms of immaterial and affective labour that are exploited in the economic circuits of the commercial web can be usefully interrogated using frameworks already identified as relevant to understanding domestic labour's role in capitalism'. Kylie Jarrett, *Feminism, Labour and Digital Media* (New York: Routledge, 2016), p. 3.

6   Federici, *Wages Against Housework*, pp. 5, 6.

7   Louise Toupin, *Wages for Housework: A History of the International Feminist Movement, 1972–77*, trans. by Käthe Roth (London: Pluto, 2017), pp. 63–64.

8   Tiqqun, *Preliminary Materials for a Theory of the Young Girl*, trans. by Ariana Reines (Los Angeles, CA: Semiotext(e), 2012), p. 15.

9   Elizabeth Gaskell, *North and South*, ed. by Angus Easson (Oxford: Oxford University Press, 1998) pp. 12–13.

10  Jane Austen, *Pride and Prejudice*, ed. by James Kinsley (Oxford: Oxford University Press, 2004), p. 29; followed by Lizzie Bennett's puncturing joke: 'I am no longer surprised at your knowing only six accomplished women. I rather wonder now at your knowing any'.

11  Tiqqun, *Preliminary Materials*, pp. 15, 17–18.

12  Tiqqun, *Preliminary Materials*, p. 17; Paul Sorrentino's TV series plays off against each other a PR-savvy, commodified Vatican and an American, ultra-conservative millennial pope.

13  Tiqqun, *Preliminary Materials*, p. 14.

14  Nina Power, 'She's Just Not That into You', *Radical Philosophy* 177 (2013) [https://www.radicalphilosophy.com/reviews/individual-reviews/rp177-shes-just-not-that-into-you].

15  Jacqueline Rose, 'Corkscrew in the Neck', *London Review of Books* 37:17 (2015) [https://www.lrb.co.uk/v37/n17/jacqueline-rose/corkscrew-in-the-neck]. The piece is a review of popular potboilers *The Girl on the Train* and *Gone Girl*, to which we might add *The Girl with the Dragon Tattoo* (film version, 2011) and *The Girls* (2017); on the implications of 2010s popular culture's fascination with sexually damaged young women, see Alex Dymock, 'Flogging Sexual Transgression: Interrogating the Costs of the "*Fifty Shades* Effect"', *Sexualities* 16:8 (2013), 880–895; for more positive academic claiming of the term 'girl', see the output of the *Girlhood Studies* interdisciplinary journal, which launched in 2008.

16  Sianne Ngai, *Our Aesthetic Categories: Zany, Cute, Interesting* (Cambridge, MA: Harvard University Press, 2012), p. 65.

17  See Susan Watkins on South American (#NiUnaMenos) and Mediterranean (#NonUnaDiMeno) forms of the movement more successfully focused on solidarity by including campaigns for greater workplace security for the precarious and political agency for sex workers. Susan Watkins, 'Which Feminisms?' *New Left Review* 109 (2018), 5–76, 60–64.

18  With paternalistic pathos and nostalgic sexism, *Preliminary Materials* declare that 'the Young-Girl reduces all grandeur to the level of her ass', (p. 37), 'the Young-Girl is not here to be criticized' (p. 39), and most tellingly, 'there is surely no place where one feels as horribly alone as in the arms of the Young-Girl' (p. 35).

19  Max Horkheimer, 'The End of Reason', *Studies in Philosophy and Social Science* 9:3 (1941), 366–388 (382).

20  Stuart Ewen, *Captains of Consciousness: Advertising and the Social Roots of the Consumer Culture* (New York: McGraw-Hill, 1976), pp. 131–149; Nancy Woloch, *A Class by Herself:*

*Protective Laws for Women Workers, 1890s–1990s* (Princeton, NJ: Princeton University Press, 2015); Fraser, 'Contradictions of Capital and Care', 105–108.

21 Siegfried Kracauer, *The Salaried Masses*, trans. by Quintin Hoare (London: Verso, 1998), pp. 53–59.

22 Stefan Zweig, *Die Welt von Gestern* (Berlin: Insel Verlag, 2013), pp. 45, 54.

23 Thomas Mann, *Der Tod in Venedig* (Frankfurt: Fischer, 1992), pp. 34–35.

24 Davis, *Women, Race and Class*, pp. 227–229.

25 Ewen, *Captains of Consciousness*, pp. 159–184, p. 182.

26 Maurizio Lazzarato, 'Immaterial Labor' in *Radical Thought in Italy: A Potential Politics*, ed. by Paolo Virno and Michael Hardt (Minneapolis, MN: University of Minnesota Press, 1996), pp. 133–146 (136).

27 Michael Hardt, 'Affective Labor', *boundary 2* 26:2 (1999), 89–100 (96); Arlie Russell Hochschild, *The Managed Heart: The Commercialisation of Human Feeling* (Berkeley, CA: University of California Press, 2012).

28 Maria Mies, Veronika Bennholdt Thomsen, and Claudia von Werlhof, *Women: The Last Colony* (London: Zed Books, 1988).

29 Paul B. Preciado, *Testo Junkie: Sex, Drugs, and Biopolitics in the Pharmacopornographic Era* (New York: The Feminist Press, 2013), pp. 285, 287, 314.

30 Srnicek, *Platform Capitalism*, p. 54.

31 Jane Austen, *Emma* (Oxford: Oxford University Press, 2008), pp. 235–236.

32 Sophie Lewis, *Full Surrogacy Now: Feminism Against Family* (London and New York: Verso, 2019), p. 24.

33 Donna Haraway, *Simians, Cyborgs and Women* (London: Free Association Books, 1991), p. 161, 166, 171.

34 Haraway, *Simians, Cyborgs and Women*, p. 151.

35  Then-Prime Minister David Cameron announced the
    Leveson Inquiry in the same month as Winehouse's death;
    there were unresolved reports that Winehouse's own phone
    was among those hacked by journalists.

36  'Director Asif Kapadia on His Moving New Amy Winehouse
    Documentary', *Vogue* 07/07/15 [http://www.vogue.com/
    article/amy-winehouse-documentary-director-asif-kapadia].

37  Diane Charlesworth, 'Performing Celebrity Motherhood on
    Twitter: Courting Homage and (Momentary) Disaster – the
    Case of Peaches Geldof', *Celebrity Studies* 5:4 (2014),
    508–510 (509).

38  We argued as much in 'For Peaches' in EDA Collective,
    *Twerking to Turking: Everyday Analysis volume 2*, ed. by
    Alfie Bown and Daniel Bristow (Winchester: Zero, 2015),
    pp. 87–88.

39  Robert Payne, *The Promiscuity of Network Culture: Queer
    Theory and Digital Media* (London: Routledge, 2015), p. 71.

40  Fleur de Force, 'Internet Famous: Fleur de Force', *Channel
    4*, 2015.

41  See Theresa Senft, 'Microcelebrity and the Branded Self' in
    *A Companion to New Media Dynamics*, ed. by John Hartley,
    Jean Burgess, and Axel Bruns (Malden, MA: Wiley, 2013),
    pp. 346–354.

42  Adorno, *The Culture Industry*, pp. 189, 191.

43  See Tiziana Terranova, 'Free Labor: Producing Culture for
    the Digital Economy', *Social Text* 18:2 (2000) 33–58; Julian
    Kücklich, 'FCJ-025 Precarious Playbour: Modders and the
    Digital Games Industry', *The Fibreculture Journal* 5 (2005)
    [http://five.fibreculturejournal.org/fcj-025-precarious-
    playbour-modders-and-the-digital-games-industry].

44  'Mother Holle' in Jacob Grimm and Wilhelm Grimm, *The
    Original Folk and Fairy Tales of the Brothers Grimm*, trans. by

Jack Zipes (Princeton, NJ: Princeton University Press, 2014), pp. 81–82.

45 Gaby Dunn, 'Get Rich or Die Vlogging: The Sad Economics of Internet Fame', *Fusion* 14/12/15 [http://fusion.net/ story/244545/famous-and-broke-on-youtube-instagram-social-media/].

46 Terranova, 'Free Labour', 53.

47 For the perils of the erosion of cultural 'gatekeepers' in the online economy, Evgeny Morozov, *To Save Everything, Click Here: Technology, Solutionism, and the Urge to Fix Problems That Don't Exist* (London: Penguin, 2013), pp. 173–180; also Andrew Ross, *Nice Work if You Can Get It: Life and Labour in Precarious Times* (New York: New York University Press, 2009), chpt. 1.

48 Alice Marwick has argued, along those lines, that social media technologies have enabled individuals to 'inhabit a popular subjectivity that resembles that of the conventionally famous'. Alice Marwick, 'You May Know Me from YouTube: (Micro)-Celebrity in Social Media' in *A Companion to Celebrity*, ed. by P.D. Marshall and S. Redmond (Hoboken, NJ: Wiley, 2015).

49 Anne Helen Petersen, 'The Real Peril of Crowdfunding Healthcare', 10/03/17 [https://www.buzzfeed.com/ annehelenpetersen/real-peril-of-crowdfunding-healthcare?utm_term=.ofvQJ1nM0#.urLaJ8xVr].

50 Luke O'Neil, 'Go Viral or Die Trying', 27/03/17 [http:// www.esquire.com/news-politics/a54132/go-viral-or-die-trying/].

51 'Amid Humanitarian Funding Gap, 20 Million People across Africa, Yemen at Risk of Starvation, Emergency Relief Chief Warns Council' 10/03/17 [https://www.un.org/press/ en/2017/sc12748.doc.htm].

52 Jean-Jacques Rousseau, *Discourse on Inequality*, trans. by Franklin Philip (Oxford: Oxford University Press, 1994), pp. 60–61.

53 Jacques Derrida, *Of Grammatology* (Baltimore, MA: Johns Hopkins University Press), pp. 165–255.

# 4 Three ways to want things after capitalism

1 Rousseau, *Discourse on the Origin of Inequality*, p. 24.

2 See Paul de Man, *Allegories of Reading: Figural Language in Rousseau, Nietzsche, Rilke and Proust* (New Haven, CT: Yale University Press, 1979), pp. 135–159; Jacques Derrida shows that the full magnitude of Rousseau's problem with history appears in *The Essay on the Origin of Languages*, where Rousseau's efforts only show that it is as impossible to distinguish a purely virtuous human before the fall into writing, technology, and civilisation, as it is to distinguish absolutely the first human from his ancestors. Jacques Derrida, 'Genesis and Structure of the Essay on the Origin of Languages' in *Of Grammatology* (Baltimore, MD: Johns Hopkins University Press, 1997), pp. 165–316.

3 Rousseau, *Discourse on the Origin of Inequality*, p. 24.

4 See de Man, *Allegories of Reading*, p. 137: 'Granted that the mode of being of the state of nature and the mode of being of the present, alienated state of man are perhaps radically incompatible, with no road connecting the one to the other – the question remains why this radical fiction ... continues to be indispensable for any understanding of the present'.

5 E.P. Thompson, *William Morris: Romantic to Revolutionary* (New York: Pantheon, 1977), p. 791.

6 J.M. Keynes, 'Economic Possibilities for Our Grandchildren' in *Essays in Persuasion* (London: Palgrave Macmillan, 2010), pp. 321–332.

7 Sigmund Freud, *Civilization and Its Discontents*, ed. by Todd Dufresne and trans. by Gregory C. Richter (Peterborough, Ontario: Broadview), p. 87.

8 Marx and Engels, *The German Ideology*, p. 57; Karl Marx, *Grundrisse*, trans. by Michael Nicolaus (London: Penguin, 1973), p. 488.

9 Emma Goldman, *My Disillusionment in Russia* (New York: Doubleday, 1923) [https://www.marxists.org/reference/archive/goldman/works/1920s/disillusionment/afterword.htm].

10 Kate Soper, 'Other Pleasures: The Attractions of Post-Consumerism' in *Necessary and Unnecessary Utopias: Socialist Register 2000*, ed. by Leo Panitch and Colin Leys (Rendlesham: Merlin, 1999), pp. 115–132 (p. 117).

11 Kate Soper, 'Marxism and Morality', *New Left Review*, 163 (1987), 101–113 (106).

12 Aaron Bastani, 'We Don't Need More Austerity: We Need Luxury Communism', *Vice* 11/06/15 [https://www.vice.com/en_uk/article/ppxpdm/luxury-communism-933]; *Fully Automated Luxury Communism: A Manifesto* (London: Verso, 2019) appeared too late for us to examine Bastani's updated ideas in detail.

13 See Robert Phelps, 'Songs of the American Hobo', *The Journal of Popular Culture* 17:2 (1983) 1–21 (6–8).

14 Thus Philip Cunliffe's scornful characterisation of FALC in *Lenin Lives!: Reimagining the Russian Revolution, 1917–2017* (Alresford: Zero, 2017), as 'the future as dreamt by under-employed, work-shy graduate students who imagine that all of life could be spent battering away on a laptop in an over-priced café in east London' (p. 120).

15  For an excellent summary of current positions on 'de-growth' and the as yet unresolved debate on whether variations on a Green New Deal would result in a contraction or a considerable expansion of living standards, see Lola Seaton, 'Green Questions', *New Left Review* 115 (2019) 105–129.

16  See Bastani, *Fully Automated Luxury Communism*, chpt. 8.

17  Slavoj Žižek, *Welcome to the Desert of the Real: Five Essays on September 11 and Related Dates* (London: Verso, 2012), pp. 11–12; on the involvement of major meat corporations in the development of new vegan foods, see Amelia Tait, 'How Veganism Went from a Fringe Food Cult to a Multibillion-Pound Industry', *New Statesman* 20/03/19 [https://www.newstatesman.com/2019/03/how-veganism-went-fringe-food-cult-multibillion-pound-industry].

18  Srnicek and Williams, *Inventing the Future*, pp. 176–177, 80.

19  Corey Pein, *Live Work Work Work Die* (New York: Metropolitan Books, 2017), pp. 22, 23.

20  Smith, *Other People's Politics*, pp. 17–18.

21  Pein, *Live Work Work Work Die*, p. 68.

22  On the notion that the present stage of capitalism already represents a 'communism of capital', see Paolo Virno, *A Grammar of the Multitude* (Los Angeles, CA: Semiotext(e), 2004), p. 111.

23  To adopt Srnicek's taxonomy, the platforms we primarily refer to here are 'advertising platforms', although our argument about their regressive logic applies in varying ways to all uses of aggregated data; Srnicek, *Platform Capitalism*, pp. 50–60.

24  Nolen Gertz, *Technology and Nihilism* (London: Rowman and Littlefield, 2018), p. 98.

25  Shoshana Zuboff, *Surveillance Capitalism: The Fight for a Human Future at the New Frontier of Power* (London: Profile Books, 2019), pp. 80–81.

26 'The aim for Facebook is to make it so that users never have
to leave their enclosed ecosystem: news stories, videos, audio,
messaging, email, and even buying consumer goods have all
been progressively folded back into the platform itself';
Srnicek, *Platform Capitalism*, p. 110; on the impossibility of
avoiding using the services of the 'Big 5' tech companies, see
Kashmir Hill's series of articles for *Gizmodo*, written over
January and February, 2019 [https://gizmodo.com/c/
goodbye-big-five].

27 From the perspective of antitrust law (governments have been
more lenient to the monopoly-seeking of digital companies
than they would be to any other kind), civil liberties
(Google's rise has been inextricable from its collaboration
with the growth of the US security state since 9/11), and
democracy (the alleged emergence of 'filter bubbles' striating
the opinions we access), to practical questions of the perverse
outcomes of the removal of human decision-making.

28 We decline for now to consider the extent to which our
critique could be applied to the assumptions about desire in
neoliberalism generally, or even capitalism as such; but an
important interlocutor text for answering that question
would be Evgeny Morozov, 'Digital Socialism?', *New Left
Review* 116/117 (2019) 33–67, especially the conclusion
(36–42) that data-based transactions in fact do not constitute
a substantially new kind of capitalism.

29 In 2016, then-UK Health Secretary, Jeremy Hunt, received
criticism for recommending patients ease the pressure on the
austerity-struck NHS by doing just that: 'if you're worried
about a rash your child has, an online alternative – where you
look at photographs and say "my child's rash looks like this
one" – may be a quicker way of getting to the bottom of
whether this is serious or not'; Ashley Cowburn, 'Jeremy

Hunt's Advice to Parents "Could Put Lives at Risk", Doctors Say', *Independent* 31/01/16 [https://www.independent.co.uk/news/uk/jeremy-hunt-s-advice-to-parents-could-put-lives-at-risk-doctors-say-a6844936.html].

30  Nolen Gertz, *Technology and Nihilism*, p. 127.

31  Jacques Lacan, *The Ethics of Psychoanalysis*, ed. by Jacques Alain-Miller, trans. by Dennis Porter (London: Norton, 1992), pp. 14, 230, 241.

32  Joan Copjec, *Read My Desire: Lacan against the Historicists* (London: Verso, 1994), p. 103.

33  Quoted, Lacan, *The Ethics of Psychoanalysis*, p. 91.

34  Lacan, *The Ethics of Psychoanalysis*, p. 147.

35  Roland Barthes, *The Pleasure of the Text*, trans. by Richard Miller (New York: Hill and Wang, 1975).

36  Alenka Zupančič, *The Odd One In: On Comedy* (Cambridge, MA: The MIT Press, 2008), p. 132.

37  It is worth noting that the working opposition we are obliged to adopt between the pleasure principle and jouissance is – as one might expect from a thinker as baroque as Lacan – not as simple as first appears. A decade after the *Ethics*, in *The Other Side of Psychoanalysis* (Seminar 17), jouissance and its opposed category have come to be formulated as much more interrelated phenomena, signalled by a preference for referring to the latter as 'surplus jouissance'. A kind of desire 'put to work' for capitalism, the potential of 'surplus jouissance' as a concept for the critique of advertising platforms has yet to be explored, although useful applications to contemporary capitalism more generally include Samo Tomšič, *The Capitalist Unconscious: Marx and Lacan* (London: Verso, 2015); and Stijn Vanheule, 'Capitalist Discourse, Subjectivity and Lacanian Psychoanalysis', *Frontiers in Psychology* 7 (2016), 1–14.

38  For a critical account of attempts to represent data aggregation as, on the contrary, a 'prophetic' kind of technology, see David Beer, *The Data Gaze: Capitalism, Power, Perception* (London: Sage, 2018), pp. 27–29.

39  Safiya Umoja Noble, *Algorithms of Oppression: How Search Engines Reinforce Racism* (New York: NYU Press, 2018).

40  For 'bad virality', a term reportedly used by YouTube employees about questionable content the algorithms nonetheless recognise as profitable and desirable, see Mark Bergen, 'YouTube Executives Ignored Warnings, Letting Toxic Videos Run Rampant', *Bloomberg* 02/04/19 [https://www.bloomberg.com/news/features/2019-04-02/youtube-executives-ignored-warnings-letting-toxic-videos-run-rampant]; for a case study of the bizarre and sometimes disgusting material produced by algorithms (and by – what amounts to the same thing – humans posing as algorithms) in the already highly-automated world of children's YouTube, see James Bridle, *New Dark Age: Technology and the End of the Future* (London: Verso, 2018), chpt. 9.

41  See Francis Mulhern, *Culture/Metaculture* (London: Routledge, 2000), chpt. 1; for a classic example of the extension of this venerable genre into the critique of digital culture, see Sherry Turkle, *Alone Together: Why We Expect More from Technology and Less from Each Other* (New York: Basic Books, 2013).

42  See Leah Price, *How to Do Things with Books in Nineteenth-Century Britain* (Princeton, NJ: Princeton University Press, 2012), p. 68.

43  Andrea Long Chu, 'On Liking Women', *n+1* 30 (2018) [https://nplusonemag.com/issue-30/essays/on-liking-women/].

44 See, for example, 'Female Erasure', *femaleerasure.com*, as pointed out by Lewis in *Full Surrogacy Now*, p. 53.

45 Andrea Long Chu, 'My New Vagina Won't Make Me Happy: And It Shouldn't Have To', *New York Times* 24/11/18 [https://www.nytimes.com/2018/11/24/opinion/sunday/vaginoplasty-transgender-medicine.html].

46 Amia Srinivasan, 'Does Anyone Have the Right to Sex?', *London Review of Books* 40:6, 22/03/18 [https://www.lrb.co.uk/v40/n06/amia-srinivasan/does-anyone-have-the-right-to-sex].

47 Where Bastani proposes communism could flourish even without the expunging of our carnivorous and capitalist desires, Chu insists on the right to gender transition, even if it leaves her present unhappiness intact.

48 Trebor Scholz, 'How Platform Cooperativism Can Unleash the Network' in *'Ours to Hack and to Own': The Rise of Platform Cooperativism, a New Vision for the Future of Work and a Fairer Internet*, ed. by Trebor Scholz and Nathan Schneider (New York and London: Or Books, 2016), pp. 20–26; Morozov, 'Digital Socialism?'.

49 Molly Fischer, 'The Great Awokening: What happens to Culture in an Era of Identity Politics?' *The Cut* 1/10/18 [https://www.thecut.com/2018/01/pop-cultures-great-awokening.html].

50 To indicate the extremes on the basis of examples from popular film, on the one hand, Jordan Peele's *Get Out* (2017) and Boot Riley's *Sorry to Bother You* (2018) have offered genuine innovations in dark comedy as a form for anti-racist and anti-capitalist art; on the other, banal superhero blockbusters *Wonder Woman* (2017) and *Captain Marvel* (2019) have been widely celebrated for their supposed revelatory feminism.

51 Producer Dan Harmon's humble and self-reflective public apology for his sexual harassment of former employee Megan Ganz (who described it as 'cathartic … like the antidote to a poison') might be contrasted with talk show host Meghan McCain's attempt to usurp the role of spokeswoman for American Jews to condemn Representative Ilhan Omar's comments on the financing of the Pro Israel lobby as anti-Semitic. See Dan Harmon, 'Don't Let Him Wipe or Flush', *Harmontown* podcast (2018), Megan Ganz, *This American Life* podcast, episode 674 (2019). For Meghan McCain, see Eli Valley's brilliant cartoon and commentary in Shuja Haider, 'Eli Valley Is Not Sorry' March 2019, popula.com.

52 'Clinton in Nevada', *The Washington Post* 13/02/16 [https://www.washingtonpost.com/news/post-politics/ wp/2016/02/13/clinton-in-nevada-not-everything-is-about-an-economic-theory/?utm_term=.be869ec17587].

53 Wendy Brown, 'Wounded Attachments', *Political Theory* 21.3 (1993) 390–410 (395).

54 Laboria Cuboniks, 'Xenofeminist Manifesto' [laboriacuboniks.net].

55 Helen Hester, *Xenofeminism* (London: Polity, 2018), p. 30.

56 Lacan, *The Ethics of Psychoanalysis*, pp. 382–400.

57 *The Point* podcast, episode 3 (May 2018).

58 Lewis, *Full Surrogacy Now*, p. 28.

59 Frase, *Four Futures*.

## Epilogue: share your limits

1 Frederick Engels, 'The Part Played by Labour in the Transition from Ape to Man' in Karl Marx and Frederick Engels, *Selected Works in One Volume* (London: Lawrence and Wishart, 1968), pp. 358–368 (359).

2  Bernard Stiegler, *Technics and Time, Volume 1: The Fault of Epimetheus*, trans. by Richards Beardsworth and George Collins (Stanford, CA: Stanford University Press, 1998), p. 113. As Marx notes on the topic of spinning machines: 'technology reveals ... the direct process of the production of [man's] life, and thereby it also lays bare the process of the production of the social relations of his life, and of the mental conceptions that flow from those relations'. Karl Marx, *Capital, Volume 1*, trans. by Ben Fowkes (London: Penguin, 1990), p. 493 n. 4.

3  Engels, 'The Part Played by Labour', p. 367.

4  Engels, 'The Part Played by Labour', p. 366.

5  Engels, 'The Part Played by Labour', pp. 367, 368.

6  Jason Moore (ed.), *Anthropocene or Capitalocene?* (Oakland, CA: PM Press, 2016).

7  David Harvey, *The Enigma of Capital and the Crises of Capitalism* (London: Profile Books, 2010), p. 85.

8  Haraway, *Simians, Cyborgs and Women*, p. 180.

9  Tiziana Terranova, 'Red Stack Attack! Algorithms, Capital, and the Automation of the Common' 08/03/14, *euronomade.info*.

10  Haraway, *Simians, Cyborgs and Women*, p. 151; Jean- Luc Nancy, *The Inoperative Community*, p. 41.

11  Jacques Derrida, *The Beast and the Sovereign, Volume 1*, trans. by Geoffrey Bennington (Chicago, IL: University of Chicago Press, 2009), p. 298; Nancy, *Inoperative Community*, p. 31.

12  Chantal Mouffe, *Agonistics: Thinking the World Politically* (London: Verso, 2013); Gilbert, *Common Ground: Democracy and Individuality*, p. 216; Walter Benjamin, 'Baudelaire [Convolute J]' in *The Arcades Project*, trans. by Howard Eiland and Kevin McLaughlin (Cambridge, MA: Harvard University Press, 2002), pp. 360–361.

# Index

# Index